HIGHLAND PONIES

AND SOME REMINISCENCES OF
HIGHLANDMEN

BY

JOHN M. MACDONALD.

FOREWORD BY

THE DUKE OF ATHOLL, K.T., P.C., G.C.V.O., C.B., D.S.O.
Lord-Lieutenant of Perthshire

J. Walter Jones, Sandringham

KING GEORGE V. WITH HIS FAVOURITE HIGHLAND PONY " JOCK."

CONTENTS

PART ONE

ISLAND PONIES.

PART TWO

MAINLAND PONIES.

PART THREE

REMINISCENCES OF SIXTY YEARS AGO.

ILLUSTRATIONS

FOREWORD

by

THE DUKE OF ATHOLL.

Mr. Macdonald has asked me to write a preface to his Highland Memoirs, more especially to that part which refers to Highland ponies.

I approach the task with some hesitation, firstly because I am a child in knowledge on the subject, as compared with Mr. Macdonald, and secondly because during the last few years I have been separated from close contact with the breed of horses which, through a long life spent in the Highlands, I have learnt to love.

It is unwise to be dogmatic about anything in this world, and especially to suggest that any human being or living animal can possibly be pure-bred in the literal sense of the term, though over a long period, if carefully bred for certain occupations, dominant strains are bound to come out, or, if put to other uses, cease to exist. To me what is termed the pure-bred Highland pony is a hybrid of long standing, built on the frame work of the North European horse, with its well-known characteristics, a dominant type that should show in every Highland pony.

On the Islands we find the breed smaller and faster and possibly nearer the original type ; smaller, partly on account of the size of the original stock and partly from underfeeding. The Island pony has

B

been used more for carrying light packs rather than
for drawing heavy weights, has had smaller mountains
to climb, less distances to go, and has been used to a
very great extent as a saddle horse. All the above
forms of work have produced a smaller, quicker type,
known as the Island pony. The best of them also
have been subject to less crossing than those of the
mainland, and where there has been any crossing, it
seems to have been with an Arab, probably a Syrian,
or with a North European horse. It, therefore, has
not gone back to worse blood than its own, but to a
strain with many of its special characteristics.

The Mainland pony, on the contrary, is a stronger
and heavier animal altogether, a type produced from
the fact that it is required for light draught purposes,
for carrying heavy weights for longer distances, over
high mountains and heavy ground.

It is a historic fact, of course, that Louis XII. of
France sent James IV. a present of a choice collection
of the best French breeds, and that James V. did much
to improve the ponies, at least in the district of Atholl.
In conversation with Mr. Thomas Dykes and Professor Cossar Ewart many years ago, I hazarded the
suggestion, which appears to have been accepted,
that some of the blood then introduced might have
been Percheron, as the two breeds had many characteristics in common, but undoubtedly, for those who
know the breed, and who have some experience, as I
have, of the Middle East, some distant but strong
strain of Arab blood cannot be concealed.

The result is that, with the Mainland pony, we
have a sturdy, somewhat rounded, muscular and
powerful animal, about 14.1 or 2 hands high,

capable of carrying great weight, with preferably a sloping shoulder, well ribbed up, not too long, strong arms and thighs, standing what I may term well four-square, flat bone, and feet not too small ; a little feather at the heels, but not hairy, like a cart horse ; tail well set on and carried free, with probably what may be termed the snow tuft at its base ; the neck strong and arched, but not too thick near the jowl ; a full mane and tail, and what may well be called a perfect head ; ears short, set up and cocked like an Arab's, bright eyes with the same characteristics and open nostrils ; wide in appearance between the eyes, probably rather dipped above the nose, a short, sensitive muzzle, and above all the air of intelligence. In action the pony should be a free walker, and when trotting should bend the knee and cover the ground, neither too high nor too low.

The oldest colours I remember, and my memory goes back to over sixty years, are black, dun with zebra marks, and brown.   Later, with the advent of the great Herd Laddie, greys predominated.   The chestnut with a light-coloured mane was looked upon with suspicion, and had no place in the Atholl stud. Of late years there has been a certain number of what I may call " dun creams," but not the mealy colour of those soft animals which used to draw Royal coaches or carry a Cavalry kettledrummer.

The breed is described as nervous, but I should rather call it highly-strung and possibly suspicious, for it fears nothing that it can understand.   From this characteristic a great many good ponies are spoilt by bad handling from men more nervous than they are, and I know of no breed of horse that is more responsive to kindness.

And what of the future ? How can we maintain the breed and where can we use it ? First and foremost as our hill ponies for sporting purposes. Every Highland proprietor ought to make it a *sine qua non* that none but Highland garrons are employed for carrying sportsmen, deer and creels. Low-set, sure-footed and sensible, they are infinitely superior for these purposes than the class of Clydesdale so easy to hire in the locality. Once it is recognised that, for the above-mentioned purposes, garrons only are required, local crofters, guides and others will not be slow to tumble to the idea. The hiring of the pony is often left in the keeper's hands, and if a garron is insisted upon, whether hired from himself or someone else, it will have a good effect on his horse psychology, especially when he realises that the average sportsman much prefers riding a garron on the hill to any other breed of animal. But to-day, when proprietors with their interest in local affairs are becoming scarcer, when factors on estates, whose owners are forced to be absentees, have little scope for sentiment, or when the control of an estate may be in the hands of a body of trustees or the like, living many miles away in the South, the maintenance of any special breed is enormously handicapped. That perhaps is the gloomy side ; the cheerful one is that the motor car or the tractor has had very little effect on the work that the hill pony has to perform, either at the plough or on the hill. Further, in these days of fewer horses in the country, I think I foresee greater scope for this wonderful breed as pack ponies in the

Army, as, in certain country, and for certain purposes, they will " see " tank and tractor every time, and when of a dun colour they will be less of a prey to the assassin of the air.

But further to maintain the breed, it is absolutely necessary that we should have first-class stallions, in which strength and weight predominate. Some means might be devised by which there should be service with selected mares only, so that the mongrels might gradually drop out. Equally it should be an offence to serve a pure-bred mare with an unsuitable stallion, and in the word " unsuitable " I include the word " Clydesdale." Service with an Arab does no harm for the purpose for which the progeny may be used, and the latter can be brought back to type again. Service with a thoroughbred, though it produces a useful roadster, is no longer required, but service with the Clydesdale produces, in my opinion, a ragged animal with a ewe neck, a long body, hairy legs and a head with long ears, a long sulky eye, a round nose and a pendulous under lip—all things not characteristic of the garron breed, though possibly virtues when brought into their proper place in a good cart horse. By careful selection we ought to get what we want, without this extraneous effort.

I fear that now I have got into trouble with Mr Macdonald so I had better stop. But, before I do, may I, as a lover of the breed, congratulate Mr Macdonald and thank him for the very excellent compendium which he has produced, and which probably he alone could have done.

ATHOLL.

PREFACE.

I was brought up with Highland Ponies and for almost sixty years they have been one of the main interests of my life. I have studied them in their native surroundings in the Western Islands and on the mainland, I have bred them on my farms in Skye and elsewhere, and I have been privileged on several occasions to judge them at the great annual shows of the Highland and Agricultural Society. Since I retired from active farming I have been looking into the history of the breed and two things have struck me—firstly, the lack of any book giving an adequate account of the history and development of the ponies, and secondly the unsuitability of many of the modern breed for the work required of them. These two considerations have been my chief incentive to write this book, and I hope that the information I have collected will have some historical value, and that my suggestions for the improvement of the breed may be considered to be of practical use—they are at least the outcome of life-long study and experience.

After I had started to write the book, I found that reminiscences of bygone days and of a state of society that has now passed kept crowding into my mind, and I decided, after much thought, to set them down in the hope that others might find them of interest. This is the explanation of the second part of this book and of its somewhat desultory nature. I might, I suppose, have arranged this part of the book more methodically, but had I done so it would, I think, have lost in spontaniety.

The compilation of the chapters on Highland Ponies has entailed a great deal of research and a mass of correspondence, and I cannot hope to name all who have been so ready to give me the benefit of their knowledge and experience. To them all I offer my most sincere thanks. I must, however, record my special indebtedness to Mr. C. R. Morrison, Mr. George King, Mr. J. H. Munro Mackenzie, Mr. Archibald Mackinnon, Mr. J. Walter Jones, Mr. Peter D. Robertson, Mr. R. Macaulay, Mr. John A. Cameron, Col. Sir Arthur Erskine, Mr. R. Ingles, Mr. Colin Campbell, Mr. Angus Cameron, Miss L. Shaw-Mackenzie, Rev. Murdo Macleod, Mr. John Stirton, Rev. A. Macdonald, D.D., Sir Alfred Macaulay, Mr. F. Low, Mr. James T. Steele, Mr. Donald MacKelvie, Mr. Geo. Laidler, Mr. Alex. Henry, Sir George Bullough, Bt., and Sir Walter Gilbey, Bt. Last, but not least, must I specially thank His Grace The Duke of Atholl for his Foreword. Owing to the Duke's long and practical connection with the successful breeding and exhibiting of Highland ponies, I feel there is no one more qualified to write this. The fact that His Grace has honoured my book in this manner speaks for itself, and to His Grace I tender my grateful thanks.

JOHN M. MACDONALD.

PART I.
ISLAND PONIES

CHAPTER I.

THE PONIES OF SKYE.

MARTIN in his *Description of the Western Islands of Scotland,* *first published in 1763, makes the following mention of the Skye ponies :—" The common work horses are exposed to the rigour of the season during the winter and spring, and though they have neither corn, hay, or but seldom straw, yet they undergo all the labour that other horses better treated are liable to do."

This description of the treatment of those ponies speaks well for the hardiness of the foundation stock— it would be pretty much a case of the survival of the fittest. However, as times changed there was a considerable improvement in the care and feeding of those ponies, and at the present day it may be said that the crofter's pony is the best cared for animal on his holding.

It is not recorded that the old proprietors of Skye took any special interest in the improvement of the breeding of the live-stock of their tenantry, and the large farmers, with one or two exceptions, were more concerned with the improvement of their sheep and paid little attention to horse-breeding. Owing to this lack of interest on the part of the people who could have afforded to introduce fresh blood, the ponies of

*Note:—A New Edition of Martin's Book was Published by Eneas Mackay, Stirling, in 1934.

Skye remained pure for a much longer period than did those of the surrounding islands, except Barra. Indeed, this applied until a fairly recent date to the east side of the island (the district of Staffin), where several ponies of note have been bred. In my young days the "east side ponies" were noted for their hardiness, and I can recall droves of them passing my old home on their way to the markets. Mouse dun and black, with occasionally cream, were the prevailing colours.

The late Lord Forteviot drove a pair of ponies from this district in one of his carriages. When, as Mr. John Dewar, he represented Inverness-shire in Parliament, he commissioned a Skye horse-dealer, who was one of his strongest supporters, to buy him a pair of Skye ponies. The dealer visited me and bought from me a black mare, 14 hands high, which I had purchased from the East Side district some years previously. This mare, along with another bred in the same district, was duly sent on by the dealer to make up Mr. Dewar's order. Years afterwards I saw those ponies being driven in a light wagonette through the streets of Perth by Lord Forteviot's coachman. They were a dead match and looked beautiful with the summer sun shining on their jet black coats. They trotted with a grace and freedom that made me feel proud of my native breed of ponies.

TWO ROAD RACES.

A former tenant of Duntulm farm (before it was put into small holdings) used to drive a pair of beautiful jet-black Highland ponies in his carriage. Those two ponies were father and son, the father having been gelded in late life, the son remaining entire. They were a dead match and very fast, and, when occasion demanded, old Duntulm made the most use of their speed. His coachman, when leaving for home from the Portree market, always got strict orders from Duntulm to pass everything he sighted in front of him, and upon no account to allow any traffic from the rear to pass him.

The tenant of Kingsburgh at that time hailed from the South and had brought with him a pair of well-bred driving cobs which were counted by many to be the fastest seen in the island for some time. On one market day, while Duntulm and Kingsburgh were having a dram together, Kingsburgh made mention of his cobs and their great pace. Duntulm, quickly jealous of anyone aspiring to possess a faster pair than he himself owned, at once challenged Kingsburgh to a race that evening on their way home from market. The marked course was to be two road miles, three miles out of the village of Portree on the road to Uig. The pace was to be that of trotting, and the leading position was to be decided by the toss of a coin. Each wagonette was to carry the owner seated behind, and the horses were to be driven by their respective coachmen. The leading position was tossed for there and then, and Kingsburgh won the toss.

The news of the race soon spread throughout the market, and that afternoon I, then in my early teens, mounted my mouse dun Highland pony, " Dunnie," and waited eagerly for the two carriages to leave the hotel stables. At last they started, and as decided earlier by the toss, Kingsburgh led. They trotted quietly out of the village, I following at a safe distance. On arriving at the starting milestone, a halt was called while Duntulm and Kingsburgh discussed matters. Soon I heard a loud shout of " Go ! " from Duntulm's powerful lungs, and away, freely stepping out, went Kingsburgh's pair of natives of the fertile Southern plains. Following not far behind came Duntulm's closely-related pair of sturdy Highlanders.

This sharp, but unforced, pace continued over the first mile of the road, while I followed in a free canter on the grass edge. On passing the first milestone Kingsburgh's strapping pair accelerated and were soon going at the top of their speed. Duntulm followed closely, and before long his ponies were breathing freely through their wide nostrils on to the tartan rug which was wrapped round Kingsburgh's legs. Kingsburgh, always a true sportsman, opened the road for Duntulm who passed and soon gained the crest of the road in front. The two sturdy natives of the island now seemed to get electrified as they tore along, stepping out as one horse. So terrific was their pace that they soon left the pair of comely natives of the South far in the rear. Immediately Duntulm passed the winning milestone he drew gently up, and by the time he had halted, Kingsburgh drew up close behind him.

Kingsburgh in true sporting fashion shook Duntulm strongly by the hand, warmly congratulating him on the mettle of his sturdy ponies. Duntulm, removing his clan tartan plaid from his broad shoulders, produced his flask, and before proceeding on the remainder of their homeward journey, they drank in Tallisker whisky to one another's good health. While the two were thus engaged, I trotted quietly past. I had not gone far when I was overtaken by the two sturdy winners of the race, who passed me at a sharp trot and looked none the worse of their last two miles of strenuous going. I had trotted behind for only a few minutes, when I was seized by a strong desire to try and out-strip them. I spurred up " Dunnie," and as I passed at full gallop, Duntulm cast a glance of strong disapproval at me. The black ponies followed me closely, and, realising this, I spurred on still faster. Soon Duntulm's ponies were encroaching upon me dangerously at full gallop, so I spurred " Dunnie " on still harder, and managed to gain slight ground. I was now fast approaching our road-end which turned off the main road with a gradual incline to the left, and before long the sight of it a short distance away aroused within me a fresh effort to get there before " Dunnie " and I were swept off the road by the pair of galloping ponies. This made me spur up " Dunnie " to her utmost speed. She responded nobly, and in a few moments we were out of danger on our own road. My feeling of immediate relief was very refreshing, especially in view of the fact that I had managed to retire gracefully from a race which I had really challenged.

I lifted my cap to Duntulm as his coachman pulled his horses up into a graceful trot. Duntulm shook his fist at me and smilingly called,

" You young rascal, some day you'll end by breaking your neck."

I again lifted my cap, and with a broad boyish smile of self-satisfaction acknowledged his warning.

LAME COLT.

My reason for giving this account of the race between Duntulm and Kingsburgh is that the entire, which was one of Duntulm's pair, has had a great bearing not only on the ponies of Skye, but also on the breed throughout the Highlands.

When Duntulm died about 1890 his farm was given up, and at the displenishing sale there was sold an entire colt which had been accidentally damaged on one of his fore-legs. Probably for that reason Duntulm had not troubled to castrate him. This lame colt was sired by the black entire which made up the pair that beat Kingsburgh; and his dam was a thick-set mare whose dam was a well-bred Clydesdale and sire a Highland pony. By his breeding he was thus two parts Highland and one part Clydesdale, and for convenience I shall refer to him as " Lame Colt ! " Duntulm's black stallion, the sire of " Lame Colt," was got by his harness companion in the race, and was sired by a Skye pony bred by the late Mr. John Stewart of Duntulm, of Highland cattle fame.

The great-great-grand-dam of " Lame Colt " on his sire's side was bought by a Skye dealer from a doctor in Lewis, nearly one hundred years ago. This mare was seemingly given to the doctor by his father-in-law as " tocher " when he married, and on selling the mare to the dealer the doctor remarked that he had got a wife and a mare at the same time, and that he found it difficult to decide which of the two was the better in their respective positions. This mare is said to have had Arabian blood in her.

To return to the "Lame Colt," he and his sire were purchased at Duntulm's sale by the tenant of Loanfern, Staffin. The sire had his leg broken shortly afterwards, and had to be destroyed. He had, however, stood at stud for several years at Loanfern, and the wide district of Staffin took full advantage of him. When mated to the small native mares of the district, this sire with his one part of Clydesdale blood, which gave him size and substance, and his two parts of real good Highland blood, seems to have acted like magic, for the results were astounding. Stout, sturdy ponies were bred, and there were many mouse dun and dark cream colours among them. Their extra size made them more marketable, especially as they still retained the characteristic hardiness of the native breed.

SOME NOTED SIRES.

One of the most noted sires which was sired by "Lame Colt" was "Rory o' the Hills." I remember when this sire was bought at Portree market by Mr. Ferguson of Talisker. He looked a most promising youngster that day. Talisker, however, owned him for only a short time, as two years afterwards he was again exposed for sale at Portree and was purchased by a south-country dealer. It now looked as if this beautiful young sire was doomed to spend the remainder of his days either down a coal-mine, or trotting through the streets of a city in a message cart. However, fortunately for the Highland pony breed, fate came to the rescue, and when "Rory" was being carried over the sea from Skye to Kyle of

C

Lochalsh in the old *Glencoe*, the Laird of Strathaird in Skye happened to be on board. Strathaird, while standing on the top deck, looking down on " Rory," was attracted by his restless vigour, and when the steamer arrived at Broadford Pier he bought him from the dealer. " Rory " was soon climbing up the gangway, and his foot was back once more on his native heath. From Strathaird he was sent to Castles on the shore of Loch Awe, and from there he found his way to the Isle of Mull, where he became the property of Mrs. Cheap (" The Squire ") of Tirroran and was used extensively.

This sire was a dark cream colour, with the characteristic black stripe along the back and black points. He was thick-set, with strong fore-arms and thighs, and I am sorry to say that at the present day it would be difficult to find many sires of the breed of the same type. He sired many Highland Society winners, and some of his sons have been used successfully by the Department of Agriculture for Scotland in their stud. The mare " Staffin Princess," which was purchased in Skye by Mr. John A. Cameron of the Land Court and shown successfully by him, is descended from " Rory." This mare is one of the best seen in our show-yards for a long time, and to my mind is the ideal type.

Another sire of note was bred at Kingsburgh in Skye, and was named " Allan Kingsburgh." This horse was sired by Stewart of Duntulm's " Skye," and was shown successfully at various shows of the Highland and Agricultural Society. He was purchased from Kingsburgh by the late Simon, Lord Lovat, the great-grandfather of the present chief

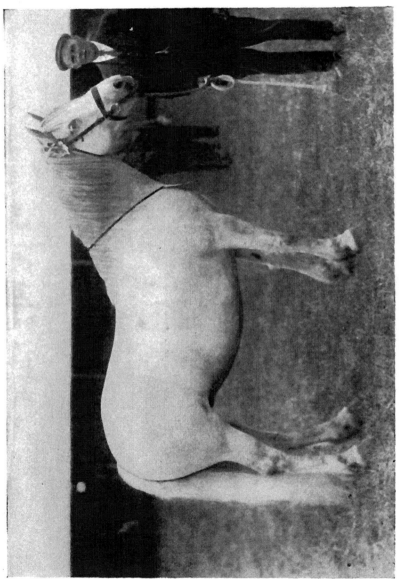

Photo. **" STAFFIN PRINCESS "** *Brown*

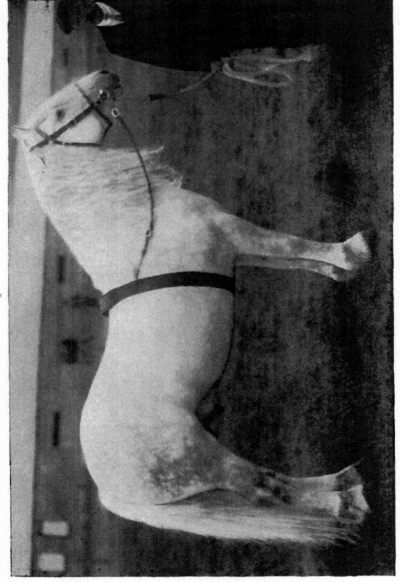

Photo.

"GLENBERNESDALE"

Brown

of Clan Fraser. Mr. Colin Campbell of Sheil, a keen and successful breeder of Highland ponies, has written to me regarding this sire : " I remember this horse well. A dark bay, thick-set and active to a degree, he was used for saddle purposes and also ran in the Castle message float between the station, Inverness, and elsewhere. Eventually he grew so thick-set and broad that they had to put wider shafts in the float. Glendoe Forest belonged to Lord Lovat. He took " Allan " across with some geldings to be used on the Forest, and parked them all in close proximity to Loch Ness. One morning when the ghillies went for the ponies, they could find no trace of " Allan " who had swum the Loch and who arrived at Beaufort Castle early in the forenoon. The Loch is a mile wide where he crossed. Lord Lovat's crofters had the use of this horse free of charge, and he left some noted stock in the Airds district of Inverness-shire."

Another sire of note, but of a later date, is " Glenbernesdale," bred by Major K. L. Macdonald, D.S.O., of Tote. He was sired by " Glenbruar," and has won the championship of the breed at the Highland and Agricultural Society's show. He was used successfully in the Duke of Montrose's stud in Arran (see page 108) and is now at the head of one of the leading Perthshire studs.

Several sires from the mainland and from Mull have travelled in Skye, but, so far as I can recall, most of them were of a nondescript class. The only sire which made a good impression on the native ponies was a horse named " Macneil's Canna." (see pp. 56 and 57). He travelled Skye in 1880, and I still faintly remember his beautiful dappled grey colour. "Herd Laddie" and "Glenbruar" are both descended from this sire, as also is "Jock," the late King George's favourite pony (see page 105). I have been told by those who remembered this horse, that he was considered the best horse that ever visited Skye.

ARABIAN BLOOD.

In 1898 the Congested Districts Board of Scotland was founded by Act of Parliament. This Board, which consisted of a secretary and a few Highland gentlemen, was formed with a view to helping the poorer districts in the Highlands. Its main object was the improvement of live-stock of all classes, and it seemed as if it might be the means of providing a brighter future for the Highland crofter. It lost no time in getting to work, and it supplied bulls, rams, and stallions to the crofters.

Professor Cossar Ewart was at this time much interested in the ponies of the various countries of the world, and he devoted much energy to breeding hybrids between the Highland pony and the wild zebra. He was successful in doing so, and I remember seeing those hybrids being exhibited at a Highland show. The Professor also claimed to have discovered what he called "the Celtic Pony," which he said was free from callosities on the hind limbs and had three varieties of hair on its tail—the short upper hair being shed annually. He gained the confidence of the members of the Congested Districts Board, and on his advice they purchased some Arabian stallions, which were sent to Skye for the use of the crofters and in the hope that they would improve the native breed of ponies. I can recall two of those sires when they were in use in Skye. They were dark bay, about 14 hands high, and had been, I think, bred in England. They were sparingly taken advantage of by the crofters who considered them too small and fine in the bone and not the least suited for the work of a croft. (Professor Cossar Ewart's experiments are dealt with in Chapter XI).

The crofters were wise in their decision. It is true that this eastern blood was responsible for our world-famous English race-horse, and it is also on record that as far back as 1712, the Chief of Clanranald imported this blood to the great improvement of the ponies of South Uist—but, the present-day crofter or small-holder does not use his pony for the same purposes as did the crofter of Clanranald's time, and on that account he needs a pony of an entirely different type. Any introduction of racing blood into the Highland ponies of to-day would, I have no hesitation in saying, be disastrous.

Those Arab sires were soon discarded by the Congested Districts Board, and years after I encountered them as geldings at local race meetings, where they showed to much better advantage than in crofters' peat carts.

After the failure of the Arabs, the next move of the Congested Districts Board was to fall back on the best procurable sires of the native Highland breed. There were not many to choose from at this period, but the Board managed to secure a few which, although typical of the breed, were much undersized for present-day requirements. The crofters, however, took full advantage of them, and it can be said that those sires helped to fix a type.

In due course the Congested Districts Board was superseded by the Department of Agriculture for Scotland which now owns a stud of typical Highland ponies and breeds its own sire for use among the crofters. (See Chapter XI.).

SAM THE " TOREADOR."

The ponies of the Island of Skye were sold at the four annual fairs held at Portree between May and November. When I was a boy I eagerly looked forward to those markets—indeed, most of the events in my young life were dated from them. I remember one event, however, that impressed me more than any other. At a September market a neighbouring large farmer exposed for sale a number of fillies ranging in age from three to five years. None of those animals had ever had a human hand upon her, and none had ever been under a roof. They were guided by an old led horse to whom they clung closely in their nervousness, and they were all strong, powerful animals. With their flowing manes and tails they seemed, to my untrained eye, to be perfect pictures.

Those fillies drew considerable attention, not only from the horse breeders and dealers, but also from the general public, and several dealers inspected them at as close quarters as they considered safe. I overheard one dealer say as he turned away,

" No sane man would risk buying those wild, unbroken beasts and having them shipped and railed to the South."

While I was standing admiring the animals, there appeared on the scene a short, sturdy man who was known to his friends as Sam. He was a horse-dealer on a large scale, and was considered to be the best judge of horses attending those markets. He was reckoned to be a " game " man and a " game " buyer. This word " game " is a true term of admiration among the dealers.

Sam examined the fillies as closely as he could, and discussed their qualities, good and indifferent, with the seller. They both retired to a refreshment tent, of which there were many at those old markets, and on their return they seemed more enthusiastic in their discussions. The seller stood erect, and with a stern look on his face held out his open palm to Sam, who quickly smacked it hard with his. They then stood for a few seconds arguing, and finally they grasped hands. This last act sealed the bargain and conveyed the ownership of the fillies to Sam.

Sam's next move was to see the fillies haltered in preparation for their journey South by steamer and rail. The old horse led them to a corner of the market square where the grass grew green and soft. Sam threw off his jacket and waistcoat and stepped as lightly as a toreador into the ring formed by the spectators. Shielded by the old horse, he quietly found his way up to the head of one of the fillies and grasped the forelock with one hand and the muzzle immediately above the nostrils with the other.

The animal gave a bound into the air, carrying the sturdy Sam with her, but when they came back to earth, to the surprise of the spectators the filly was stretched flat on the ground with Sam kneeling beside her and pressing her neck into the soft grass. Willing hands slipped a halter over her head, Sam released the pressure on her neck and stood back, and the filly, springing to her feet and with the halter dangling from her head, found her way back among the unhaltered animals.

The same procedure was adopted towards the next animal, and though this one seemed more difficult to take to earth, in the end Sam managed to get her down. This went on till the last of the fillies was haltered.

Sam was the hero of the market, and to one admiring boy at least he gave a thrill which the great Rodeo at Wembley many years later failed to give.

CHAPTER II.

THE PONIES OF UIST.

THE islands of South Uist, Benbecula, and North Uist are separated from one another by the sea only at high tides. They contain wide stretches of machair land along the whole of their western coasts, but the land along their eastern coasts is rocky and heather-clad and less adapted to cultivation. At a period not far distant most of the best land was in the hands of large farmers, but since the Government took up land settlement, those large farms have been turned into holdings. On that account the increase in the number of small holdings in those islands must be very large.

CLANRANALD'S SPANISH HORSES.

The ponies of those islands have changed considerably in type from time to time owing to the influence of outside blood. In the early days, when ploughs and carts were not in use, those ponies were pretty well left to roam over the hills, and allowed to breed at random. The first record we have of any interest being taken in them is in *The History of the Hebrides and Highlands of Scotland*, written by John Walker, late Professor of Natural History in the University of Edinburgh. Professor Walker mentions that the Chief of Clanranald, who was killed at the

Battle of Sheriffmuir in 1715, had been a Colonel in the Spanish service, and had, on his return home not long before 1715, brought with him some Spanish horses which he settled in his principal island of South Uist. To a considerable degree these altered and improved the horses in that and in the adjacent islands.

Even in the year 1764, not only the form, but the cool, fearless temper of the Spanish horse could be discerned in the horses of South Uist, especially in those in the possession of Clanranald, and of his cousin, Macdonald of Boisdale. At that time, those ponies, both by build and disposition, were thought to be the best horses in the Highlands, and although of low stature, they were judged more valuable than other horses of the same size.

HEBRIDEAN PONIES IN 1811.

In 1811, Macdonald in his *Survey of the Agriculture of the Hebrides* wrote :—

" The Hebridean breed of horses resembles that which we find in almost all countries of the same description of climate and surface. It is small, active, and remarkably durable and hardy. In general, the tenants pay no manner of attention to the stallions and breeding mares, but leave them almost entirely to chance. In summer and early in autumn, one half of those horses and mares range freely and unconfined amidst the mountains, whence they are not brought to the different farms and hamlets for work until the harvest is ended, the crop to be carried home, and the peat and fuel to be secured. They are then hunted after like so many wild beasts, and each tenant or proprietor endeavours to secure his own, which he has not seen for many weeks before. They are driven into enclosed pens or fields, frequently into bogs and morasses, before they can be laid hold of, and sometimes they are injured severely in the process. Their manes are then cut, the hair laid up for rope-work or other purposes, and the young horses are gradually broken in for the labour and cruel hardships of the winter."

IMPORTED STALLIONS.

At a later period, some of the proprietors imported stallions of various breeds. The late Mr. John Gordon, proprietor of South Uist and Benbecula, imported, in the early eighteen seventies, a grey Arabian stallion for the use of his crofters. This horse might be given some credit for having a refining influence on the ponies of those islands, but this influence cannot be said to have tended to maintain their hardiness, although some of his descendants, bred out of the larger mares owned by farmers, were noted for their speed, those out of the small mares belonging to crofters were ill adapted for the work they were called upon to do.

In the eighteen nineties Sir Reginald Gordon Cathcart introduced a pair of Norwegian stallions of a chestnut colour. Those horses were much better suited for the stormy and wet climate of the islands, but they did not improve the native breed in any way, though they maintained its hardiness. There had previously been in Uist ponies of a chestnut colour with silver manes and tails, but those Norwegian stallions added considerably to their number.

The only Clydesdale of which we have any record was introduced by a contractor, but of this I shall have more to say later in the chapter. It is sufficient to state here that this Clydesdale seems to have been a most successful sire, producing the type of pony which the crofter found best for his purposes. When he was mated with the small native mares, the foal was without fail a stout, sturdy animal, strong in bone and with a thick-covering of hair which is absolutely necessary for protection from the prevailing strong westerly winds. Some of the first of those cross-bred foals were kept for breeding and were mated to native mares with very good results.

HORSE BREEDING IN UIST.

The islands of North Uist, South Uist, and Benbecula are well suited for the breeding of horses, and the natives are very fond of riding—indeed, it is said that a Uist man will walk a mile to fetch his horse so that he may ride that same distance on an errand ! There used to be many horses bred there, but after the slump in prices, the crofters ceased breeding. Since prices have improved, however, breeding has again increased.

Formerly all the stock was sold at markets held in July and September, but now public auction sales are held by various firms of live-stock salesmen. I attended the markets as far back as 1892, going by steamer from Skye to Lochboisdale, attending on successive days markets in each of the three islands.

MARKETS AND LUCKPENNIES.

There were many amusing scenes at those old-world markets. Dealers from the South and from Aberdeenshire attended them and bought strings of ponies, mostly yearlings but with a sprinkling of older horses. It was an interesting sight at the close of a market day to see the dealers with bulging pocket-books surrounded by small crowds of sturdy crofters. A projecting stone amongst the heather served as an office stool, and the man of wealth sat thereon and doled out sheaves of pound notes in payment of the various purchases he had made earlier in the day. After each crofter had received his money, the dealer invariably demanded a " luckpenny," and a long, and sometimes hot, argument ensued, the dealer maintaining that he had paid far too much for his purchase. In the end the crofter usually returned into the dealer's hand a coin which was accepted with the remark, " faur o'er little." While this coin was still in the palm of his right hand, the dealer always spat on it with considerable force. He then conveyed it with a good deal of flourish into his trousers pocket. I understand that this insanitary old custom must never be omitted or the good luck will be broken !

After all the payments had been made, the next move was to get the young, unbroken colts haltered. This was usually done by the dealer himself with the assistance of some of the crofters. When the haltering was finished, about half a dozen of the colts were tied head to tail and the leader was tied to the tail of a strong and steady horse. It was often a wonder to me that the tail of this leading horse, with six sturdy colts pulling wildly on it, did not come out of joint. Many horses must, indeed, have sustained some bodily hurt. For example, a friend of mine who had bought a very good-looking pony at one of the markets, thought to save expense by lending him to a dealer to lead his string of colts to Lochmaddy for shipment to the South. In due course the pony arrived home, but it was much exhausted by the journey, and it never properly recovered.

AT THE FORDS.

Another interesting sight at the time of the fairs was the driving of the live-stock across the ford between Benbecula and North Uist. In good summer weather and at the height of spring tides, this ford can be crossed almost dry-shod, but in September and later months during strong westerly winds and at neap tides, there remain, even at low water, channels containing considerable depths of water. Under these latter conditions I have seen hundreds of shaggy Highland cattle and many Highland ponies, mounted and in strings such as I have described, surrounded by scores of wild-looking islanders, both mounted and on foot, with dogs barking fiercely all bent on forcing their droves across the waters of the ford. The difficulty was to get the leading cattle to enter the water—once they had done so, the rest followed without much trouble.

I have stood on the vast stretch of white sands, through which flows the salt water river that joins the Minch and the Atlantic Ocean, and watched droves of cattle plunge into the water until nothing could be seen of them but their shaggy backs and long horns. The drovers followed them on foot, after taking off their lower garments, tying them into tidy bundles, and hugging them under their arms. Their nailed boots were tied together by the laces and hung round their necks. The water at its deepest covered the men close up to their ribs, and at this point they always took the precaution of hanging on to the tail of the nearest pony or cow.

The riders on horseback, often two on the same pony, also plunged into the water, lifting their legs high to save a wetting. Carriages drawn by two horses, dogcarts, gigs, and crofters' carts were all packed to their utmost carrying capacity, for it is a recognised rule never to refuse a " lift " to anyone wanting to cross the ford.

This ford with its wide expanse of innocent-looking white sands is not always as entertaining as it was to me on this particular September afternoon. Many people have been drowned there, usually when crossing at night. It is said that on moonlight nights there is often to be seen a form of mirage which mis-leads travellers and makes them lose their way.

GRADING UP THE BREED.

In finishing my observations on the ponies of those islands, I should point out that for several years the Department of Agriculture for Scotland has been supplying Highland pony stallions for the use of the crofters. Those sires are of a good stamp and are true to the Highland type, and I think I am safe in saying—though some of my friends will not agree with me—that they have had a good influence in helping to grade up the ponies. The only complaint made by the crofters is that the sires are too small and that on that account their progeny are through time going to be unfit for the work of the crofts.

Many of the crofters who have been settled on the large farms that have been broken up into holdings, are now anxious to secure horses of a larger size. The land they have under tillage is more extensive and of better quality than what they had formerly, and so also are the grazings. The small pony that was suitable for the work on the miserable patches among the rocks, is now quite unfit for the larger holdings. The crofters need and want to breed bigger ponies, and it is the duty of the Department of Agriculture for Scotland to supply larger sires of a stronger type. This is a subject to which I shall return later. (See Chapter XII.).

BAIN'S STALLION.

I have mentioned the influence of Clydesdale sires on the Uist ponies. I have vivid recollections of one of those horses. After the passing of the Education Act of 1872 school-houses were built all over the Islands, the work being done by contractors from the South. One of those contractors, who came from Ayrshire, brought with him to Uist a thick-set, dark brown Clydesdale stallion to do the carting for him. For a number of years this horse worked at the various buildings throughout the Island, and at the same time the crofters were allowed to use him for breeding. The number of foals he left must have been very considerable, and he made a good impression on the native pony stock.

Many well-known Highland pony sires can trace their ancestry back to this Clydesdale, which was known as " Bain's Stallion "—Bain being the name of the contractor. One of them was the pony sire " Moss Crop " which was bred at Balranald in North Uist, and which, when owned by Mr. Donald Stewart of Drumchorry in Perthshire, won the gold medal at Dumfries Highland Show in 1903 and was first at Aberdeen Highland Show in the following year. This horse was sired by " Sollas," which was bred by Mr. Morrison of Sollas in North Uist, and " Sollas " in turn was sired by " Bain's Stallion."

Mr. Thomas Dykes, in an article on the Highland Pony in the *Transactions of the Highland and Agricultural Society for* 1905, describes " Moss Crop " as of an old North Uist strain, and gives his dimensions as—height 14.2 hands, below the knee 8½ inches, thigh 21 inches below the hock, width between legs 10½ inches. In 1904 " Moss Crop " served eighty mares of all sizes from 12 to 16.2 hands in Inverness-shire and Perthshire, and almost as many in 1905 in Inverness-shire, Perthshire and Forfarshire.

Another pony sire of note descended from " Bain's Stallion " is " Islesman," which, when owned by the noted Mull pony breeder, Mr. J. Munro Mackenzie of Calgary, won first prize at the Highland Show at Dumfries, in 1903. This pony was got by a sire known locally as " McCormick's Stallion," which was bred in Benbecula and sired by " Sollas." " Sollas," as we have seen, was got by " Bain's

D

Stallion." Mr. Dykes says of this sire :—" An excellent representative of the modern Mull pony is ' Islesman,' first prize winner at the Highland and Agricultural Society's show at Dumfries in 1903. He has plenty of bone, good joints and feet, and possesses pleasing shapes."

While those two sires, " Moss Crop" and " Islesman," can claim to have the best of Uist blood in their pedigrees through their dams, we cannot but admit that the Clydesdale blood obtained through " Bain's Stallion " must have added considerably to their substance. They both have had a great influence upon many of the best ponies of the present day.

AN UNEXPECTED ARRIVAL AT VATERSAY.

When the building of the Uist school-houses was finished, " Bain's Stallion " was taken on board the steamer at Lochmaddy to be shipped back to the South. One of the passengers happened to be a relation of mine, who was tenant of the island of Vatersay, near Barra, and who was returning from his honeymoon. Before the ship was long away from Lochmaddy, the contractor succeeded in selling the old horse to him.

The Captain of the ship had agreed to land Vatersay and his wife in the bay below his house, but unfortunately a full gale blew up from the southeast. I was a small boy at the time, and along with my elder brother was staying at Vatersay. We naturally went down to the shore to welcome the honeymooners, and with us was the faithful " *Iain Ruadh* " (Red John), Vatersay's grieve. He was a man of medium height, with wide shoulders and strong chest, and he had a bright red beard and hair of a slightly duller shade. His clear blue eyes with their quick glances showed signs of an alert mind and a quick temper, both of which he possessed to a strong degree. When he was roused, his vocabulary of Gaelic oaths was wide and complete.

We three stood on the shore, for it was impossible to launch a boat, and watched the steamer heaving on the rough seas. In a short time, and when still a good distance out, it came broadside on opposite the place where we were standing. A door in the side was flung open, and to our amazement we saw the old horse being pushed over. In an effort to save himself he gave a great spring as he was leaving the deck, and then with a plunge he disappeared into the sea.

We all held our breath for we thought we had seen the last of him. In a few seconds, however, he appeared on the crest of a large wave, and we saw that he was swimming strongly for the shore. In a very short time he was on dry land and slowly walking on to the white sand. He stood for a moment or two, and then shook himself. I watched him closely, and as I was used only to Highland ponies, I was struck by his " immense " size (as a matter of fact, he was not more than 15.2 hands).

He next lifted his head high, and, sniffing the air, gave out a loud neigh. The four farm horses were, as was then the custom, tethered not far away, and when they replied in chorus, the old horse set off at full gallop in their direction. *Iain Ruadh* followed, but the horse outstripped him.

The old warrior was soon careering among the
farm horses, with his ears back and his mouth wide
open, showing his long yellow teeth. He plunged
about wildly and uttered such sounds as I have never
since heard outside a zoo. In the end the four horses
pulled their tethers and galloped away with the old
horse close behind them.

Iain Ruadh was now quite out of breath, partly
from the exertion of following, and partly from the
strain of uttering Gaelic oaths against his master for
having let loose so ferocious an animal in this peaceful
island.

Both *Iain Ruadh* and the old horse soon quietened
down, and Iain worked him for many years on the
farm. In the breeding season, he travelled Ardnamurchan, Strontian, and Morvern, and left many good
foals.

CHAPTER III.

THE PONIES OF BARRA.

THE Island of Barra, the largest of the more southerly islands of the Outer Hebrides, was once famous for its ponies. The island was owned by a long line of the Chiefs of the Clan Macneil who were renowned for their kindness to and consideration for their tenantry. Martin in his *Description of the Western Islands of Scotland* says of those chiefs :—

" If a tenant chance to lose his milk cows by the severity of the season, or any other misfortune, in this case Macneil of Barra supplies him with the like number that he lost."

The Chiefs seem also to have been interested in the improvement of the native ponies, and it is said that they introduced Arabian stallions for that purpose. One of those stallions must have possessed great beauty and speed, as it inspired one of the Islands bards to write of it in Gaelic verse ; he described him as " Macneil's milk-white steed with flowing mane and tail and surpassing in fleetness the stags of the forest."

ARABIAN BLOOD.

The Macneils were notorious pirates—for this crime one of them, indeed, suffered a long term of imprisonment and in the end, I think, the death penalty. It is said that the Arabian stallions which were brought to Barra were " lifted " from a Spanish ship.

The increase of size, which must have taken place on the introduction of Arabian blood at this early period, cannot have been maintained at the time of Dr. Johnson's tour of the Hebrides, for, after mentioning the Rhum ponies (see p. 50), he refers to the Barra ponies as follows :—

" There are said to be in Barra a race of ponies yet smaller of which the highest is not 36 inches."

THE ANNUAL DRAFT OF FOALS.

On account of the isolation of Barra the ponies remained uncrossed for a longer period than in any other part of Scotland. As late as the nineties of last century a relation of mine, who then farmed the extensive island of Vatersay as well as some of the neighbouring islands, bought a drove of foals, some times forty in number, from Barra every autumn. He sent them to winter on a small island where they got nothing to eat but what they picked, and I remember being taken as a small boy to see them there. The shepherd rounded them up with his dog like sheep, and brought them at the gallop close up for his master's inspection. They were of various colours with coats fully three inches long, and many of them had small Arab-looking heads with the small sharp ears protruding from a mass of hair, and a thick-growing forelock. Each spring my relation sold the whole draft to two men from the south who came to the island for that purpose and who shipped them to Glasgow and then exported them to America.

This annual sale ended in rather a peculiar way. The purchasers always insured the ponies heavily to cover the risks of the sea voyage to America, and on one occasion they arranged with the man in charge of them that he should poison them during the time they were on board ship. He did so, but the insurance company was suspicious, the plot was discovered, and the criminals ended by serving long terms of imprisonment.

DESCRIPTION OF BARRA PONIES.

At that time (the end of the nineteenth century), few of the Barra ponies were over 13 hands in height, but they had fine clean bones and joints, small Arab-looking heads, and many of them were sprightly and most attractive in appearance. They were much sought after by people in Skye and on the mainland for driving in pony traps, and many of them had great staying powers and speed. Some of them, indeed, attained great speed in a pacing gait.

I once owned one of those ponies which I picked as a foal out of a large drove bought by a dealer in Barra. He was a red chestnut in colour, with mane and tail of a lighter shade. I let him run unbroken till he was rising five years old, and this, along with the good grazing, helped him to grow to fully 14 hands. He often covered the twenty-four miles from my farm to Portree in a little over two hours, and he could jump a fairly high hurdle or a wide ditch with the greatest of ease. I sold him to the proprietor of the Sligachan Hotel, and he in turn sold him to an Englishman who broke him to play polo and used him in many important matches.

CROSSING WITH UIST PONIES.

At one time the crofters of Barra had no carts and used their ponies solely for creel work. As old roads were improved, however, and new roads made, and as the size of crofter holdings increased they found that their beautiful ponies were too small for their needs. They then imported stout Uist ponies, with the result that the native breed is now almost extinct, or has been crossed with larger sires sent by the Department of Agriculture for Scotland. This has resulted in a good class of pony with more size, but with the characteristic hardiness of the native breed. I understand that on the Island of Eriskay, adjacent to Barra, there are still to be found a few of the native ponies of the old type.

A VANISHED SCENE.

As a boy I once saw, winding their way in single file through a glen, about a dozen of those native Barra ponies laden with creels full of peats. They were guided by fresh-complexioned girls who were clad in brightly striped skirts of home-made drugget, and who had their heads and shoulders wrapped in bright clan tartan shawls. Such a scene will never again be witnessed, unless some film-maker will find his way to this distant island and make a picture of " Barra Sixty Years Ago." He would still find the glen and the old track unchanged, but

BARRA PONY WITH PANNIERS

might have difficulty in making up the rest of the picture.

A HISTORICAL NOTE.

The well-known writer and clan historian, Dr. Archibald Macdonald of Kiltarlity, has written to me as follows :—

" I have in my hands an old Roup Roll of the effects of Roderick McNeil, Tacksman of Sandra, Barra, showing the prices fetched by live-stock in 1783. Eight horses were sold at an average of £2 a head, sixteen yeild cows were sold at £1 4s per head, fifteen two-year-old queys at an average of 11s 5d. I suppose the horses were the real old Barra breed of native ponies."

CHAPTER IV.

THE PONIES OF RHUM.

RHUM ponies were famous even before the days of Dr. Johnson who mentions them in his *Journey to the Hebrides.* Boswell and he were the guests of the Laird of Coll, a Maclean, who also owned Rhum, and according to *The Statistical Account of Scotland* Rhum in those days had a population of 300 but owing to the unsuitability of the land for cultivation and the production of food, there was great poverty. Maclean, who was a kindly and sympathetic landlord, seemed much concerned about his tenants, and although he was fully alive to the advantages of emigration, he had not the heart to enforce it as many other landlords of the time did. By the end of the eighteenth century, however, the force of circumstances was such that the people had of their own free will emigrated to foreign lands.

Dr. Johnson's mention of the ponies of Rhum is as follows :—

" The ponies are very small but of a breed eminent in beauty. Coll not long ago bought one of them from a tenant who told him as he was of a shape uncommonly elegant he would not sell him but at a high price, but that whoever had him should pay a guinea and a half."

It would thus seem that, in the eyes of the natives of the other Hebridean islands, the breed had a special value for improving purposes.

RHUM PONIES IN ENGLAND.

A former Marquess of Salisbury bought Rhum in 1840, and at that time there were ponies running wild on the island. Sir Walter Gilbey in his book *Thoroughbreds and Ponies*, refers to them as Black Galloways. In his book, *Ponies Past and Present*, the same author quotes a letter from Lord Arthur Cecil, son of the Marquess of Salisbury, in which he stated : " I think what interested me so much in those ponies was that as long ago as I can remember anything, I heard my father describing them to old Lord Cowley and the Duke of Wellington. He told them how like the Spanish horses he thought the ponies in 1840, and mentioned how he had turned down a stallion on the island. He also said that he saw no reason why they should not be descended from the Spanish Armada horses which were wrecked on that coast.

" When the ponies, most of them stallions, came to Hatfield in 1862, I remember some of them broke out of the station and it took several days to catch them again. They were almost unbreakable, but my brother, Lionel, and I managed to get two of them sufficiently quiet for us to ride, though they would not have been considered safe conveyance for an elderly gentleman. We were never quite sure of their ages, but they must have been nearly thirty when they died.

" I believe my father intended to keep those ponies entire, but they were so hopelessly savage that they had to be cut. They could trot twelve

miles in fifty-five minutes after they were twenty
years old, and could gallop and jump anything in the
saddle."

Lord Arthur himself took an interest in the New
Forest ponies and brought down some Rhum
stallions with a view to improving that breed.

Sir Walter Gilbey quotes another letter from
Lord Arthur :

" The Rhum ponies, which were much thought
of by my father, seem to be quite a type by themselves, having characteristics which would always
enable one to recognise them anywhere. Every one
of those I bought in 1888 had hazel-nut brown eyes,
and, though only a small boy in 1862 when six or
seven of those ponies came to Hatfield, I remember
that they also had the hazel eye. They have almost
without exception very good hind quarters with tail
well set up, and it is in this respect that I hope they
will do good in the New Forest."

Lord Arthur also makes mention of having bought
a Highland pony stallion from Coulmore in Ross-
shire to head his Rhum stud. This pony was mouse
dun with black eel stripe, and was sired by " Allan
Kingsburgh," to which I have referred when dealing
with the ponies of Skye (see p. 27).

IMPROVING THE BREED.

In 1888, the father of the present proprietor,
Sir George Bullough—of racing fame—bought
Rhum from the Marquess of Salisbury, and
at the same time took over the stud of ponies. At
various times Sir George sent some of his mares to
England to be served by one of Lord Arthur Cecil's

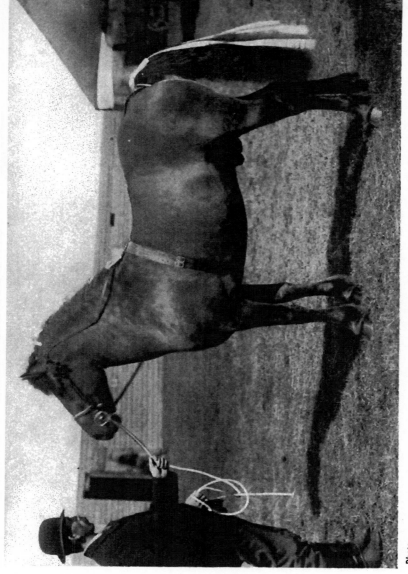

Reid

" CLAYMORE "

Photo.

Highland pony stallions which still represented the old Rhum strain of ponies. From time to time, too, Sir George has purchased the best types of stallions, among the most noted of them being "Claymore," which was bred at Strathaird in Skye and got by "Rory o' the Hills." He won first prize at one of the Highland Shows.

I visited Rhum in 1920 and saw a good number of the ponies in one of the gloomy glens of the rugged island. There were a good many mouse duns and some chestnuts with silver manes and tails. Few of them were over 14 hands. I was deeply interested, especially as I knew that the same strain has been in the island for centuries.

SHEEP AND DEER.

At one time the Island of Rhum was famed for its blackfaced sheep, the three-year-old wedders being considered among the best sold at Inverness Wool Fair. But the sheep have now all been cleared off, and the island is given over to deer. At the time of my visit I was much struck by the large size of the deer. This, I was informed, was due to the frequent introduction of fresh blood from England. Those imported stags arrive enclosed in strong crates and with their antlers off close up to their skulls.

THE WELSHMAN'S CLIFF.

On the occasion of my visit to Rhum I sailed round the island, and the boatmen pointed out to me an immense cliff which rose almost perpendicularly out of the sea. Along the face of this cliff, half-way up but still several hundred feet above the sea, I could make out a narrow sheep or deer track, running right across it. There was room neither for two animals to pass on meeting face to face, nor for one of them to turn, and as a result I am told, in the old days many sheep and deer were killed here. The mortality was especially heavy during the rutting season of the deer, when stags often meet and engage in a combat which ends with one or both of them falling into the sea several hundred feet below.

When the Marquess of Salisbury was proprietor of the island, he resolved to widen the track, but no one in Scotland could be found to undertake this dangerous job. In the end he engaged half a dozen slate quarriers direct from Wales and they soon had the work completed. This great cliff is now known as *Creag-a-Wealishech*—" The Welshman's Cliff."

AN ANCIENT STUD.

In the hands of Sir George Bullough, the present owner of the island, the Rhum stud has won many honours at the shows of the Highland and Agricultural Society. An old groom, Duncan Macinnes, who left the island in 1931, has told me that at that time there were twenty-six ponies in the stud, and that most of them were dun in colour. Long may this stud remain pure, and long may it flourish, for no other stud of the breed has such an ancient record.

CHAPTER V.

THE PONIES OF MULL.

THE island of Mull has been noted for its ponies from a very early period. It is said that the ponies there, like those of Rhum, benefited from the horses which swam ashore when vessels of the Spanish Armada were wrecked on the West Coast of Scotland in 1588. Martin in his *Description of the Western Islands of Scotland,* which was published in 1695, says of the Mull ponies :—" The horses are but of a low size, yet very sprightly."

A VETERAN'S REMINISCENCES.

Mr. C. R. Morison of Kengharair in Mull who is now over eighty years of age and who is keenly interested in the old breed of Mull ponies, his forebears having farmed on the island for generations, has given me a good deal of information and has written to me as follows :—

" In regard to the Mull ponies, I have been brought up among them and was fairly fortunate in always having a good one. With us in Mull we had the two classes of ponies—the small or Island pony was known as *Gocan,* and the other was, in my opinion, purely and simply the Galloway breed. Both of them were beauties. The *Gocan* class were disappearing in my young days, and the other class were taking their place.

" The first entire I remember was a brown horse called ' Duncan.' He belonged to my uncle, but was standing at our farm, Treshnish, in 1864. I remember him well, as he was the first horse I have any recollection of riding. In 1864 he was tethered in a field near the house, and I often heard my father say that he left sixty foals that year. He was about fifteen hands, and a perfect model. He was the sire of ' Polly,' a beautiful black mare of about the same size, and ' Polly' was the dam of ' Macneil's Canna ' (see pp. 27 and 106).

" The sire of ' Macneil's Canna ' was a grey horse that Mr. Campbell of Ulva had out of a Highland mare and an American horse called ' Yankee ' which was brown in colour and about fifteen hands in height—a perfect demon to handle. ' Yankee ' was the property of Mr. Campbell, the Duke of Argyll's factor in the Ross of Mull." The groom who travelled ' Macneil's Canna ' in Skye in 1880, tells me that ' Yankee ' was brought from America by Mr. Campbell's brother who was the captain of a sailing ship.

" I had," Mr. Morison continues, " the second foal that ' Macneil's Canna ' left—a rare model and as strong as a rock. He was a great cart horse and was equally good in the trap. I also had a full sister of this horse, and she too was a perfect beauty. My father, who used to ride her, was very proud of her and gave her every care. Mr. Mackenzie of Calgary was for years in the habit of hiring a pair of horses on the show day, and when the grey pony was 28 years old she passed this pair going to the show and then left them a long way behind. Mr. Mackenzie was as happy as a lord over it."

GOCANS.

" In regard to the *Gocans*, I think that the crofter evictions helped to do away with them. They were hardy and could live out all winter. In spring when work began they might get a sheaf of corn, and also when the snow covered the ground, but at other times they had to do for themselves. They were excellent ponies for the crofters—they carried everything in creels, getting the peat home in season, and also carrying the sea-ware and the potatoes. When the cart was introduced, the *Gocan* kicked against it, finding it too heavy.

" My father had a grey *Gocan* for riding, and I remember seeing him trying it in the cart. It lay down and would not move, so he took it out, gave it a good thrashing, and then got it into the cart again. It just lay down once more.

" The other class of ponies was, as I have already said, almost certainly the *Galloway*. Some of them, I should say, were 15 hands high, and they were thick and short in the back.

" In the seventies and eighties of last century my cousin managed the Marquess of Northampton's Mull estate and had to buy big Clydesdales for the heavy carting. My grey horse would take a hole more in the girth than any he had. This grey horse was out of a brown Ross of Mull mare by ' Macneil's Canna.'

E

" As to the word *Gocan*, I am sure you have heard of *Gocan na Cuthag*. The ground lark when it follows the cuckoo is always known in Mull as *Gocan na Cuthag*, and I have often heard the phrase applied to a small, conceited man. I think it would be used of the Mull ponies on account of their smallness of size and of their conceit and their determination to keep up with the larger ponies. They could keep going on the road for any distance.

" My father often told me about his *Gocan*. Once he left Treshnish in the early morning and went round our parish, a distance of over forty miles (my father was Inspector of Poor and weighed over 14 stones). On his way back he was met by my uncle who had to go to Edinburgh on urgent business. My uncle said, ' I must take a lad with me to bring back my pony from Grasspoint, and I have no pony available for him to ride.'

" He can take ' Tammy,' " my father said.

" The poor *Gocan* had then to go off other twenty-eight miles to Grasspoint, and when he got there he was as fresh as the other pony and perfectly fit to return home.

" I have always been interested in the Mull ponies and have constantly advocated the keeping up of the breed, but long ago I saw that they were doomed—latterly, weight was all that was wanted, even although it took a pair of big Clydesdales to keep themselves in oats. The uncultivated farms of Mull prove the mistake that was made."

LORD DOUGLAS'S HORSE.

About 1870 a Mr. Lang of Glengorm in Mull
introduced two horses of the old-fashioned roadster
or hackney type, "Lord Douglas" and "Tom
Thumb," both of them fast trotters. The first
named was a brother of the celebrated champion
"Douglas," which, in his day, was invincible on the
trotting tracks. The sire of those "Douglases"
was the famous chestnut stallion known in the West
of Scotland as "Lord Douglas's Horse."

The father of the Duke of Hamilton, then the
Marquess of Douglas, being in London and in a hurry
to catch a train, hailed a hansom cab. He was
struck by the smartness of the horse's performance
and asked the driver to whom it belonged. On
being told, he made arrangements to buy him, and
he was sent first to Hamilton Palace and then to the
Island of Arran, where he stood for two years at
Brodick Castle. The Duke presented him to his
tenant, the late Mr. James Allan of Balnacoole, who
let him in 1854 and 1855 to Mr. William Caldwell
of Boydstone, Ardrossan, at £15 a season. He got
the two colts mentioned above. He was put down at
Balnacoole at the close of 1855, three years before his
extraordinary merits as a sire had become fully
recognised.

"Lord Douglas," Mr. Lang's horse, died in
1876, and some of his descendants are still to be found
in Ayrshire and the Island of Arran, but there are
very few in Mull. This is explained by the fact that
the popularity of the Douglas blood was so great in

the West of Scotland that everything bearing the name and showing merit was bought privately.

As an instance of the reputation of "Lord Douglas," I may state that Mr. Allan was offered by a prominent hackney breeder £5 for a hoof with a shoe on it, if he could unearth it from the horse's burial place in Balnacoole stackyard.

From some information I once received, I was led to understand that "Macneil's Canna" was descended from "Lord Douglas," but on further enquiry I find that this was not the case.

THE CALGARY STUD.

No one in the Western Isles, at least within the last fifty years, has taken more interest in the breeding of Highland ponies than has Mr. J. H. Munro Mackenzie of Calgary. With a view to improving the native breed, he bought an Arabian stallion, "The Syrian," from Algiers. Mr. Thomas Dykes in his article on THE HIGHLAND PONY in *The Transactions of the Highland and Agricultural Society for* 1905 quotes a letter from Mr. Mackenzie in which he says :—

"The line I am going on is to try and get better backs and shoulders on the Highland ponies. I like the Clydesdale as much as any man, but the cross was not a success. I am crossing Highland mares with "The Syrian," a well-bred and very good type of Arab. I am putting the fillies of the cross back to "Isleman." Putting "The Syrian" to very small ponies, 12.2 to 13 hands, I got the foals too small, but putting him to strong Highland mares, about

14.2 hands, I have had some grand ponies, and all I have sold have averaged £40 each. I am quite sure the Arab blood has made the Mull ponies what they were in the old times, and I do not see why they should not go back to them again."

Mr. Mackenzie, through this mating, had fixed a type of his own that became known in the show-yards as the Calgary type. They were beautiful ponies of their kind, showing, through the influence of Eastern blood, more breeding than the ordinary Highland pony, They were in much favour in the show-yards of our national shows, especially after the South African War when the country became alive to the need for hardy and active remounts with a fair turn of speed, which would facilitate advance or retiral in the field.

The craze for the Calgary type left the breeders of the sturdy garrons very dissatisfied with their success in the show-yards, and as a result, the Highland and Agricultural Society was called upon to have two classes—Highland Ponies and Western Island Ponies.

Great credit must be given to Mr. Mackenzie for having fixed a type of riding Highland pony, through the careful intermingling of Western Island, Garron, and Eastern blood. His ponies have found a ready and profitable market, principally in the South. At the Newcastle Royal Show in 1935, Miss Mackenzie (Calgary's daughter) showed two ponies with which she won first and reserve in a big class of mountain and moorland ponies of all breeds—Fells, Dales, and others—all shown in saddle.

THE DEPLETION OF THE BREED.

After the Galloway ponies of the South had been crossed out with the Clydesdale and other breeds, dealers found that the nearest available supply of ponies of this type was in Mull. They flocked to Salen Fair, where not only were the Mull ponies sold, but also those from Coll and Tiree and the adjacent parts in the mainland. The demand for those strong, sturdy horses soon depleted that area of its best types of the native breed. This process was hastened by the introduction of the Clydesdale by the south-country farmers who at that time found their way to those islands and rented farms. Soon the native breed disappeared, and with the exception of Calgary, no one now seems to take much interest in their breeding.

CHAPTER VI.

THE PONIES OF ARRAN.

THE island of Arran was, as we have already seen (in Chapter V.), the home, for a good part of his life, of the famous " Lord Douglas " to which many of the modern bred hackneys can trace their ancestry. Although this horse cannot claim to have had any influence on the present race of Highland ponies, two of his sons were used in Mull, as has been explained in chapter V. The tempting prices offered for their progeny by dealers from the South soon depleted the island of all the Douglas blood. It is difficult to say what influence this strain might have had on the Highland pony if it had been used in a judicious manner.

At the present day there is in Arran one of the most enthusiastic of Highland pony breeders, Mr. Donald MacKelvie. He has had a stud for over twenty years, and has shown successfully at the various Highland and Agricultural Society's Shows during that period. The foundation of his stud was laid by the purchase of mares from North Uist, two of these being " Macdonald's Betty " (5363) and " Moss Jean " (3604). Others of his mares were " Jess o' the Glen " (3605), a mare descended from an old Skye strain, and " Kilbride " (4137). The famous " Glenbruar " (see p. 64) was exchanged with Rosehaugh in 1923 for " Glenscorrodale," Mr.

MacKelvie's first stud horse. Mr. MacKelvie says
that he has never had any reason to regret the trans-
action. This horse stamped his type on every foal
he left, and soon brought Mr. MacKelvie into the
first rank of Highland pony breeders. He supplied
many of the leading pony studs with " Glenbruar's "
sons as stud horses, and exported others to foreign
countries, including Palestine.

Mr. MacKelvie writes me as follows regarding
" Glenbruar " :—

" I think there is no doubt that ' Glenbruar '
was the most impressive sire of his time ; he had a
wonderful constitution, and no constitutional weak-
nesses that I was able to discover, and you know that
I inbred him very closely. ' Glenbruar ' had to
be destroyed in September, 1931, as his hind-quarters
became paralysed. As I have probably told you, three
colt foals were born to him in that year—' Ruarie,'
bought by Sir William Cross ; ' Bennan,' shipped
to Palestine ; and ' Gleann,' still in my possession."

The Duke of Montrose keeps a small but select
stud at Brodick Castle, but in recent years his ponies
have not figured much at Highland and Agricultural
Society's shows. " Glenbernesdale," a son of
" Glenbruar " and a champion of the breed at the
Highland Show, was the last stud horse which the
Duke had in use.

THE RENOWNED " GLENBRUAR "

CHAPTER VII.

THE PONIES OF LEWIS AND HARRIS.

It does not seem as if many ponies have ever been bred in the islands of Lewis and Harris. The reason for this probably is that there the crofter holdings are small patches situated amongst the rocks close to the sea-shore, and that the soil has of necessity to be turned by the ordinary spade or by the old-fashioned *cas-chrom*.

In his *Description of the Western Islands of Scotland* Martin makes the following note about the ponies of Lewis :—

" The horses are considerably less here than in the opposite continent, yet they plough and harrow as well as bigger horses, though in the spring-time they have nothing to feed upon but sea-ware."

About 1840 the mare from which " Rory o' the Hills " (see p. 24) is descended, was (as I have related in Chapter I.) purchased from a doctor in Lewis by a Skye dealer and brought to Skye.

Professor Ritchie in his book on *The Influence of Man on Animal Life in Scotland* says, " We can safely assume that the bones of a very small horse found in the ancient underground ' Pict ' or ' Erid ' house at Nisibost in Harris, are those of the earliest known representative of the European race."

CHAPTER VIII.

THE PONIES OF TIREE.

THE island of Tiree was once the stronghold of the Highland pony, or, as it is termed in Mull, the *Gocan*. In Macdonald's *General View of the Agriculture of the Hebrides*, published in 1811, it is stated that, " The Island of Tiree keeps 1500 ponies or nearly as many as the great Isle of Skye, which is twenty times its superficial extent, at least 10 times its value, and maintains nearly seven times its population. All kelp islands keep swarms of horses to the great hurt of other stock."

In the seventies of last century, a Clydesdale sire was introduced to Tiree by a Mr. Barr, who rented several farms in the island, and from that time the native breed of ponies began gradually to disappear. In recent years the large farms have been divided up into crofts or small holdings, and on that account horses have increased considerably. For the last few years the Department of Agriculture for Scotland has, at the request of the smallholders, sent a Highland pony stallion for use on the island, and I have no doubt that the cross between the Clydesdale mares and the Highland sire will bring home the advantage of keeping a medium-sized horse, that will do their work equally well and will save about fifty per cent. in the cost of food.

CHAPTER IX.

THE PONIES OF ISLAY.

THE enthusiasm which is now applied to the breeding of Clydesdales in Islay, was at a very early period devoted to the breeding of Highland ponies. Writing of the Thanes of Cawdor in his book *Scotland During the Middle Ages* Cosmo Innes says :—" Somewhat more care is shown in the breeding of horses. Long before this time the Lairds of Glenorchy had introduced English and foreign horses for their great stud in Perthshire, and the example was followed in Cawdor." Probably, too, the example was followed in Islay for as early as 1638 Duncan Campbell, writing from Islay to his brother Colin of Galcantray, says, "I wyshe if you may Cromarties old Spanish horse provyding he be of a reasonable prys."

At a much later period, James Macdonald in his *General View of the Agriculture of the Hebrides,* written in 1811, says, " About thirty years ago there were no carriage roads and not above two or three carts in the whole island of Islay. Young horses were broken by yoking them by their tails to harrows. Mr. Campbell of Ballinaby has a regular succession of Gerrans for the plough, cart, and saddle. For all purposes this answers extremely well. He rears them accordingly from dams of various forms and sizes, but an uncommonly handsome middle-sized stallion which is fit for any of the above-mentioned purposes, and he gets almost any price he demands for his young colts. Twenty-five, thirty, and even forty guineas are no uncommon price for Islay garrons, 11, 13 to 14 hands high, and numbers of them are exported each year even to Galloway and Ireland."

At the present time there are few if any Highland ponies in Islay, although at a recent period Mr. Morrison, the proprietor of most of the island, kept a useful stud.

CHAPTER X.

SHETLAND PONIES.

IT has long been thought that Shetland possessed a native pony before the Scandinavian invasion and settlement of the ninth and subsequent centuries.

While some of the Shetland ponies of the present day (especially those on their native Islands) closely resemble the Norwegians, there are others which belong to a different type with fine shoulders and fine bone, and with small Arab-looking heads. These characteristics are not apparent in the Scandinavian breeds, and the fact that they appear in the Shetland pony is evidence of another ancestral strain. This is clearly shown by the fact that the Shetland ponies of this Arab or oriental type do not form a distinct type within the breed, but crop up here and there.

The existence of this oriental type is put down, like many other influences on the different breeds of horses, to the horses off the Spanish Armada. The modern type of Shetland pony may be said to have been descended from the stud founded by the Marquess of Londonderry in the Island of Bressay, Shetland, in 1870. The Marquess of Londonderry being an extensive coal-owner in Northumberland, the ponies were bred originally with a view to using them as pit ponies. The formula of the stud, therefore, was to get ponies as near the ground as possible, with as much weight as could be got.

Within a comparatively short period this low but strong type of pony was arrived at by Londonderry, and by skilful selection most of the defects of conformation which were common among the island ponies were eliminated. This source of improvement—as in so many other breeds—can mainly be traced to a single animal, "Jack" (16) foaled in 1871, which came into Lord Londonderry's possession as a colt and was the sire or grandsire of almost all the stallions used in the stud, as well as a large proportion of the mares belonging to it. The success of the noted sire was partly accounted for by careful in-breeding both of himself and his sons and grandsons. As an instance of this form of successful in-breeding "Lord of the Isles," a son of "Jack's," when mated to his own dam, produced the renowned stallion "Multum in Parvo."

The Londonderry Stud was broken up in 1899, and at twelve Highland and Agricultural Society Shows previous to that date it carried off all the leading honours.

The Londonderry ponies were of the type to which I have referred earlier as the Scandinavian type or, when talking of Highland ponies, "Garron type." Soon however, a craze developed among some of its breeders to develop what may be called a riding type of Shetland pony, and this meant the development and improvement of the oriental type referred to earlier. The chief source, of which we have any record, through which this oriental or riding type of pony was procured was through the influence of the noted sire "Prince of Thule." This sire had the necessary characteristics—

a long rein and high withers with an Arab-looking head, which helped to fix a type entirely away from the pit pony type bred by Londonderry.

Owing to the introduction of electric haulage in coal mines the need for the employment of Shetland ponies has almost disappeared, with the result that the only market now left is that of supplying children's ponies, so that there is a good deal now to be said in favour of developing this type. It is commonly thought that the ponies of Shetland were individually made small by the severity of the conditions under which they lived, that they were and are dwarfs, stinted by starvation. But this is not the case, as ponies reared in southern climates and on the richest of pastures show no tendency whatever to increase in size. As already mentioned, the market for Shetland ponies has practically disappeared, and this might be the reason why in recent years the D.O.A.S. were called upon by the Shetlanders to let them have the service of one of their Highland pony sires, which has been in use there for several seasons. The cross between the Highland pony and the Shetland mares will serve a purpose for which the small native ponies were not adapted, but will not in any way make them lose their hardiness.

PART II.

MAINLAND PONIES

F

MAINLAND PONIES.

THE Highland ponies of the mainland are sometimes called " garrons," and although this name properly means " gelding," it is now generally applied to the strong, sturdy, small horses which hardly come under the title of ponies. This class of sturdy animal is also to be found in the Islands, but as it is there a product of crossing, it can hardly be called a native breed.

In the Board of Agriculture and Fisheries' pamphlet on *British Breeds of Live-Stock* occurs the following :—

" The Highland garron is the largest (14 to 15 hands) and strongest of all pure breeds of ponies in the country and is admirably adapted to the work of carrying the sportsman to the hill and returning with heavy loads of deer, up to 18 stone weight, from the wild forests of the Scottish Highlands."

Garrons have been described as having good game heads, bold eyes, shoulders a bit straight, good legs and feet, tufts of hair on the heels, and often a very well set on tail. Although there is no historical record of the fact, it is more than probable that they are descended from Percheron stallions which were mated to useful but small Highland ponies, for Louis XII. of France sent James IV. " a present of a choice collection of the best French breeds." James V. in 1535 passed a law " for increasing the size of the Scottish horses and more particularly those of the ancient Scottish forests of which Atholl is one of the oldest." These efforts at improvement were continued, and confirmatory evidence of this is found in the fact that foals of grey Highland mares are born black or dun in colour with a silver hair through the foal coat which is replaced in the adult by grey hair.

GALLOWAYS.

Highland ponies or garrons were referred to in the South of Scotland as Galloways, and Sir Walter Gilbey in his book on *Thoroughbreds and Ponies* says, " Galloway ponies were used for pack work, as oxen were used for ploughing."

Even before the commencement of the nineteenth century, this animal, which cannot be described either as a horse or as a pony, played an active part in agricultural work in the Lowlands of Scotland in localities where no roads existed. Galloways were used both for riding and for the transport of agricultural produce, but they lacked the weight and strength to draw the heavy two-horse ploughs. Ploughing was done by oxen, but the sleighs which took the place of carts were drawn by Galloways and they also carried a good deal of general merchandise in panniers.

The original Galloway was generally under 14 hands in height ; " Youatt " (second edition, 1846) says, " it varied from 13 to 14 hands, though it was sometimes more, and it was a bright bay or brown in colour, with black legs and small head. The purposes for which it was used indicated the desirability of increasing its strength and height, and with this in view cross-breeding commenced shortly after the beginning of the nineteenth century and continued till almost 1850. As a result, the old Galloway has disappeared from all parts of the mainland of Scotland and survives only in such remote situations as the Isle of Mull." " Youatt " could not have had an intimate knowledge of the Highlands and Islands or he would not have confined the Galloway or Highland pony to the Island of Mull at as late a date as 1846. In point of fact, at that time Highland ponies in the West Highlands and Islands and in the higher districts of all the Highland counties were purer bred and more numerous than they are at the present day—and this despite the Stud Book and the keen interest that is now taken in the breed.

CHAPTER I.

THE ATHOLL PONIES.

Mr. Thomas Dykes (pp. 41 and 42) says of the Atholl ponies :—

"Undoubtedly the Atholl ponies have a very ancient history, though the early part of it has not been recorded. In 1540 Henry VIII. sent to the Scottish King, whose favourite hunting and hawking quarters were the Forest of Atholl, under Sir Ralph Sadler, his ambassador, a number of Spanish jennets and Barbary horses which were evidently intended for breeding purposes. James IV. had previously introduced into Scotland several Spanish stallions, and Louis XII. had presented him with twelve of his choicest French horses, no doubt the grey horses of Normandy. Most likely, breeding operations in Atholl were seriously disturbed, as they were in Glenorchy, by the rebellion of 1715. Still, the old strain was seemingly never allowed to die out, though, mayhap, changes of blood were introduced from time to time.

"We have exceedingly pleasant mention of these ponies, some of which were models for Landseer's pictures, in Queen Victoria's *Journal of our Life in the Highlands.* Writing on 18th September, 1842, when she was the guest of the Duke of Atholl at Blair Castle, Her Majesty says, 'We set off on ponies to go up one of the hills, Albert riding the dun pony and I the grey, attended only by Sandy McAra in his Highland dress. We went out by the back way across the ford, Sandy leading my pony and Albert following closely, the water reaching above Sandy's knees.'"

PONIES OF THE SCOTTISH HORSE.

" On the occasion of King Edward's visit to Edinburgh in 1903," says Mr. Dykes, " we had, on the invitation of the Marquess of Tullibardine, the pleasure of going over the representatives of the Atholl Stud which were in Edinburgh as mounts for members of the detachment of the Scottish Horse. Four were greys, one a stylish mare, winner of first prize at Ballinluig Show, almost white, one a dun, one a dapple-brown, and one a chestnut. The dun mare with eel back stripe, bred by Mr. Macmillan of Calvine, had much true Highland pony character and has won leading honours wherever shown. The greys were more interesting, having been bred at Blair for many generations A notable representative was the Duke of Atholl's favourite hill-pony, ' Tommy,' now going on for thirteen years. He has great, powerful loins and quarters—in fact, is a miniature dray-horse to whom a sixteen-stone stag would be but a featherweight. The daily hill journey at Forest Lodge during the season, we were assured, is rarely under thirty miles. The white mare, scarcely so powerful as ' Tommy,' is of the same build and shape."

LORD TULLIBARDINE'S NOTES.

" Since the formation of his regiment, Lord Tullibardine (now Duke of Atholl) has taken the greatest interest in everything pertaining to the Atholl stud, and he has been good enough to supply us with the following notes :—

" ' With regard to the Atholl stallions, the earliest of which I have a record, was a piebald. No record exists as to the sire of " Morelle," which was foaled in 1853 and described as a true garron. " Morelle " was destroyed in 1872, having had one colt foal in 1871.

" ' The first stallion of the recorded stud was " Glentilt," foaled in 1862 and grey in colour. He was bought from Donald Cameron, Glengarry, Inverness, for £13 10s, and sold to the Earl of Southesk in 1869 for £60. He was the sire of several of our best hill ponies, notably " Lady Jean " in 1867. " Lady Jean," who was afterwards used as a brood mare, had as her dam " Polly," a garron mare bought from Mr. Halford, the tenant of Foss, who bought her in Muir of Ord market. In 1868 " Polly " produced to " Glentilt " the dun colt " Glengarry." This colt was kept as a stallion, and was the sire of many good animals before he was sold in 1879 to Mr. J. C. Cameron, Garrows, Glenquaich.

" ' " Glengarry II." was our next stallion. He was by " Glengarry I." out of a garron mare bought at Inner Hadden, Rannoch. The next stallion was " Herd Laddie," foaled in 1881. He has been the most successful stallion we have had, and is still going. We have a young one coming on after next year, called " Bonnie Laddie," which is by " Herd Laddie " out of " Minette." " Minette " is one of the best brood mares that ever was in the Atholl Stud, and is by " Glengarry II." out of " Minnie,"

"LADY LOUISE"

a yellow dun foaled in 1861 by a cream-coloured garron, name unknown.' "

THE ATHOLL STUD TO-DAY.

My own earliest recollections of the Atholl country are of the days when the Atholl fold of Highland cattle was at the height of its fame, and the two magnificent bulls, " Calum Riabhach" and " Calum Ban," were making the history of their breed. At that time the Atholl stud was, as I have already said, of considerable standing, and this it has maintained right down to the present day. For this it has to thank the influence of " Herd Laddie."

I saw " Herd Laddie " when he was shown as "extra stock," at the Highland and Agricultural Society's Show at Edinburgh in 1907. He was then twenty-six years of age and snow white, but his vigour and action as he pranced round the ring put the rest of the ponies to shame. He was bred in Lochaber and sired by " Highland Laddie " who, in turn, was sired by " Macneil's Canna," a beautiful dappled grey which I saw when he travelled in Skye in 1880 (see pp. 56, 106).

One of " Herd Laddie's " most famous sons was " Bonnie Laddie " which was bred in the Atholl stud and which the Marquess of Tullibardine mentions in his notes (p. 80). He gained the championship of the breed and the special prize presented by the Polo and Riding Pony Society for the best male at the Perth Highland and Agricultural Society's Show in 1904, and in the following year he was again champion at Glasgow. I think that I

am justified in saying that most of us who remember
this pony are agreed that he was the best type of
pony that we ever saw. He was just the standard
height of 14.2 hands, was light dun in colour with a
black eel stripe along his back, and had strong bones
of the best quality and perfect feet and legs. It
would have been impossible to improve upon his
head with its prominent crest, his long, sloping
shoulders, his deep, well-sprung ribs, his short-
coupled and beautifully turned quarters, and his
perfect movement both at the walk and at the trot.

The most renowned female in the stud at this
time was the beautiful mouse dun, " Lady Louise,"
who was champion at the Highland Show at Paisley in
1913. Two of her daughters were also champions—
one at Edinburgh in 1907, and one at Dumfries in
1910.

In recent years the Atholl stud has not been
showing, but Mr. R. Inglis, the Factor, tells me that
it is still at the same high standard of efficiency, the
present stud horse being " Beinn Odhar," a great
grandson of " Herd Laddie," and winner of the
Paisley Perpetual Gold Challenge Cup at Inverness
in 1923, the only occasion on which one of the Highland and Agricultural Society's special trophies was
ever given for competition by Highland ponies.

THE CIRCUS PONY.

An incident which illustrates the weight-carrying
capacity of the Atholl ponies may here be recorded.
Once when I went to a performance given by a travelling circus, my attention was drawn to a Highland

Photo. "BONNIE LADDIE" Reid

pony of the real garron type. This grey gelding, slightly over 14 hands in height, was of the real Atholl type—low and long, with great, strong loins and quarters and strong fore-arms and bone. He acted the part of what is known as a " back rider ; " that is to say, with his back well dusted with resin (invisible) to prevent the riders' feet from slipping, he galloped round the ring carrying various performers in all kinds of ways. He concluded his " turn " by carrying seven full-grown people (five women and two men) at a free and light gallop round the ring. Taking the average weight of the seven riders at 8½ stones, this pony was carrying at least sixty stones, and he did not seem to feel that this was causing him the slightest exertion.

I afterwards asked Mr. Inglis, the Duke's Factor, about this pony, and he wrote me as follows :—

" I have been to Fosset's Circus and seen ' Billy,' the Highland pony about whose wonderful carrying capacity you wrote me, and I agree with all you say. Whenever I saw the pony I remembered him quite well. He was sold in Perth Market and bought by Naismith of Glenfarg. His sire was ' Bonnie Laddie ' and his dam was a grey mare, ' Skye Linnet,' which was bought from Mr. Peter Robertson of Castlecraig. She was sired by ' Atholl ' and her dam was ' Skye Lark.' "

" Billy's " carrying feat certainly shows the capabilities of a pony built on the proper weight-carrying lines.

CHAPTER II.

THE APPLECROSS STUD.

THE late Lord Middleton, who owned extensive estates at Birdshall, near York, was not only a noted breeder of shires and blood horses, but on his Highland estate at Applecross he also kept a very select stud of Highland ponies. In his breeding of all classes of livestock he was both enthusiastic and practical, and he gave the following particulars about his Applecross stud to Mr. Thomas Sykes who quoted them in his article on the Highland Pony in the *Transactions of The Highland and Agricultural Society for 1905.*

"The present Applecross stud," said Lord Middleton, "was formed about the year 1878, though previous to that time my father, the eighth Lord Middleton, kept and bred ponies at Applecross. About that time he came into the possession of a grey mare, ' Kitty,' which he bought along with the property from the Duke of Leeds in 1861. This mare had been bred by the Mackenzies of Applecross who had ponies at the time which had been bought in Skye. The mare ' Kitty ' was a good type of the Highland pony.

"In 1878 I bought a bay mare in foal from Mr. Macrae of Glenvargil in Skye. He (Macrae of Glenvargil) was of the same family as the Macraes of Camasunary near Loch Coruisk in Skye. This mare was a beautiful type of Highland pony, small, strong, and full of mettle. At that time she was in foal to a pony that took first prize at the Highland and Agricultural Society's Show. She dropped a bay filly, and she and this filly now go by the respective names of ' The Old Skye Mare ' and ' The Young Skye Mare.' From these two mares many of my ponies have been bred.

" In 1882 I bought a beautiful grey mare, ' Molly ' (foaled in 1872 or 1873) at the sale of Lord Dacre's ponies at Garve, Lord Dacre having given up his forest. She was his favourite hill pony. I also bought another mare which did not breed. This mare, ' Molly,' was larger than the two Skye mares— about 14 hands and strong. She had a family of three colts and two fillies to ' Glen,' whose sire used to travel in Skye and was a chestnut with a white mane. The eldest colt, foaled in 1884, was a chestnut with silver mane and tail. I have ridden him for the last fifteen years and have always taken him with me to Scotland. He is a wonderful pony—up to sixteen stone, can walk five miles an hour, is exceeding wise and clever, and never makes a mistake. A sister (grey in colour) was a carriage pony and is breeding now, while another sister travels at Birdshall with the stallions. A brother goes in harness. The other colt I sold.

" In regard to types and colours, all my ponies are thick-set, strong, short-legged, and bred especially for carrying weights such as the carcases of deer, and for riding on the hill. Their colours are black, chestnut, grey, and bay—the chestnut having probably come in from ' Glen ' as I hold that chestnut and black are akin. In the spring the ponies plough, cart, and execute the general work of the foresters' crofts, and in the autumn they do the work required of them in the forest. Some of them I use as carriage ponies, and some I employ at Birdshall for going messages to the Post Office and the like, or for travelling as the grooms' mounts with the thoroughbred and shire stallions.

" All the ponies are brought to Birdshall to be broken, usually arriving in a truck along with the Highland cattle. They are then broken at the hunter stud farm and used for the different classes of work already alluded to in order to make them quiet and tractable. Those required for work at Applecross are returned there as needed.

" I have successfully bred some ponies at Birds-hall from an Arabian stallion—beautiful, hardy ponies fit for polo or for use as hacks and, I should think, just the sort for mounted infantry. I have all through tried to keep up the Highland pony hardihood. Here at Birdshall and at Applecross, they only get hay or silage during the snow times, but, of course, during the stalking season they get a daily feed of corn. They are never under cover, except the carriage horses, and even they are turned out for the winter."

The first sire used at Applecross was, as we have seen, " Glen," a black or brown pony bred and owned by Mr. Macleod of Coulmore, which, incidentally, is in Ross-shire, near Kessock Ferry, and not in Skye as some writers have asserted—it was at one time rented by the Macleods of Kingsburgh in Skye. " Glen " was of the same blood as " Allan Kingsburgh " (see page 27), and was a strong, thick pony with capital feet and legs and good shoulders. He was bought by Lord Middleton in 1881 and died in 1888.

The next stud horse at Applecross was " Fitzgeorge " (4265), born in 1877 and sired by " Sir George " (778), the famous champion prize-winner owned by Mr. Christopher W. Wilson of High Park, Kendal. " Fitzgeorge's " dam was " Fanny," a well-known Cumberland mountain mare of good Fell stock. He was bought for Lord Middleton at the Islington show in 1893, and was a grey, 14 hands in height, of great power and substance, and with very good action. " Borrodale," a grey by " Fitzgeorge," and foaled in 1895, was a strong, thick pony with good action, out of " Morag," a wonderfully good, strong dun mare of beautiful type which was used for many years on the hill. " Morag's " dam was sired by a dun pony out of the old grey mare, " Kitty," and her grand-dam was the " Old Skye Mare." The dun pony was by " Comet," a Welsh pony which belonged to Mr. Bower who rented Strathaird in Skye, and which travelled that island and left a lot of good stock.

" Borrodale " was bought by the late Mr. John Robertson of Fodderty, Strathpeffer, and was shown by him at one of the Highland and Agricultural Society's shows, where he won first prize. Mr. Robertson eventually sold him to an English breeder.

As will be seen, Skye blood has always been strong in the Applecross stud, and when crossed with the blood of " Sir George," who was a blend of Fell and Hackney, it produced a very good type of pony.

In regard to the breeding of the noted " Sir

George " type of pony, I cannot do better than quote the following from a letter written by the late Mr. Christopher W. Wilson of Rigmadden Park, Kirkby-Lonsdale :—

" The old Galloway was the same as the Fell pony, only it showed a little more breeding. The Fell pony in my part of the country is from 14.1 to 14.2 hands in height and is used for all kinds of farm work—in fact, it is a cart cob in miniature. The Arab crosses will not stand the winter out of doors. I saw a lot of them in the Island of Harris, but they could not remain out in winter as do the Fell ponies. No doubt the Arab cross sweetens their heads, but they lose the bone and constitution. My ' Sir George ' ponies used to lie out all winter, and I only took them up about three weeks before sending them to the Islington Spring Show, where I frequently won with them. I am quite sure that the Hackney would be a much more suitable cross for the Fell pony to breed troopers from than is the Arab. The resultant ponies would be much hardier. I don't, of course, mean the pampered-up hackney."

A VISIT TO THE APPLECROSS STUD.

I inspected the Applecross stud about the year 1910. It was a dull February afternoon when I landed off the steamer on the shore of Applecross Bay, but the manager, who was a very great friend of mine, welcomed me in true Highland fashion. Next morning we inspected the ponies, most of which were low and long with long hind quarters, high set on tails, well-developed thighs and fore-arms, and ample strength of bone. There were a few blacks and browns and many duns and greys, and my host told me that those ponies had often to carry sportsmen of over seventeen stone across the roughest and softest of hill ground. Often, too, the stags that they had to bring down from the highest corries exceeded that weight. I must say that the ponies looked well equal to those tasks.

I purchased their stud horse, " Grenetote," a dark brown, strong son of " Islesman," who had been bred in North Uist and who had won a first prize at a Highland and Agricultural Society's show. I also bought two beautiful grey mares.

Next morning when I was due to return to Kyle of Lochalsh, a strong north-westerly gale was blowing into the Loch and the steamer was unable to call. As the road across the hill to Strathcarron was blocked with snow, it was obvious that I could not get home till the weather moderated. As a matter of fact, I was held up for three days, but I do not think that either the manager or myself was sorry at the opportunity of spending a little more time in one another's company.

My host took me up to the mansion house to see the trophies of the chase, and we spent a long time looking at the rows of stags' heads round the walls of the hall. Some of the heads were the finest that I have ever seen, and on the mounting board of each was a neat brass plate recording the date when shot, the name of the successful sportsman, and the weight of the animal.

One exhibit, however, interested me more than did the stags' head—this was the mounted head

G

of the famous Highland bull, " Leoch." This bull
had been used in many of the most noted herds of
Highland cattle, and had ended his days at Applecross.
He was bred on the Island of Ensay off the coast of
Harris, by the renowned breeder, Mr. John Stewart
(see page 196), who, after winning the championship
with him at the Highland and Agricultural Society's
show, sold him for £300 to another noted breeder,
the Earl of Southesk.

The Earl had a passionate love for his cattle,
and his manager, Mr. Donald Fletcher, told me that
two days before his death he ordered him to parade
them before his bedroom window so that he might
have a last look at them. After they had all passed,
the Earl waved his hand to Mr. Fletcher and to his
faithful cattleman, Donald Macphail, and was then
helped back to the bed from which he was never again
to rise.

" Leoch " was probably the finest Highland bull
that has ever been bred. He was of a golden yellow
colour and had a magnificent head and horns. When
he was not in too high condition he weighed one ton,
one hundredweight, and even at that great weight
I have seen him stepping lightly round the show
ring with his head held high. Strangely enough,
although he himself was such a fine animal, he never
bred any stock of note and, indeed, most of his off-
spring were decidedly plain looking. This brings
home the uncertainty of stock-breeding, and reminds
me of a story told me by an Englishman who rented
a shooting near my farm.

A LESSON IN HUMILITY.

This Englishman was a bookmaker, and his calling brought him into contact not only with race-goers, but also with horse-breeders and hunting men. One of these last with whom he was very friendly commissioned him to purchase a hunter, and owing to his great weight the cost of a horse that would carry him in comfort and safety ran to several hundreds of pounds.

Some time later the bookmaker met his friend and asked how he was pleased with the hunter. He replied that he was thoroughly satisfied, but that, owing to the cost, he had decided to breed his own hunters in future and had already bought a few of the best mares available and was about to mate them to the best hunting sire in England.

Many years afterwards the two men met again, and not unnaturally the bookmaker asked how the horse-breeding was getting on. His friend looked at him more in sorrow than in anger and replied, " If you want to be taught humility, breed horses."

Then he walked away without any further conversation.

CHAPTER III.

GLENARTNEY FOREST STUD.

THIS stud, which belongs to the Earl of Ancaster, was founded about the year 1870. The late Lord Ancaster leased for a time the Forest of Gildermory in Ross-shire. On the expiry of the lease there his Lordship brought his ponies to Glenartney. The first sire in use in this stud was " Young Glengarry," probably a son of the Atholl-bred "Glengarry I." Since then there have been seven different Highland sires in use and at the present time an experiment is being tried by crossing a few of the mares with a " Dales " pony. This pony stands over fourteen hands high with great bone, fine long riding shoulders with a long rein and small pony head, and also a very correct mover. This experiment is of very great interest and should be closely watched by Highland pony breeders.

At present the stud numbers round about 100 head, and is one of the largest in the country. Considerable business is done in hiring out ponies for the moors and forests during the shooting season.

CHAPTER IV.

THE PONIES OF SUTHERLAND AND CAITHNESS.

ALTHOUGH there are no Highland pony studs in the County of Sutherland, the crofters and small-holders, especially those along the west and north coasts, use Highland ponies for their work, and the Department of Agriculture for Scotland sends out several stallions to travel the district.

Over thirty years ago the Duke of Sutherland owned a Highland stallion named " Lord Reay," which was bred in Caithness and which left a strain of typical ponies throughout that part of the country. At the outbreak of the Great War, the Duke had a number of well-bred ponies for use in his forests, but they were all taken over for War purposes ; Sir Alfred Macaulay, the Duke's Agent and Factor, tells me that they were to be returned if wanted, but that none ever came back. Probably, like most of the pre-War deer forest ponies, they are now buried in Gallipoli and on the plains of Flanders.

In his book on ponies Sir Walter Gilbey says :—

" About the end of the eighteenth century a Mr. Gilchrist employed on his farm in Suther-landshire as many as ten garrons to carry peats from the hill and seaweed from the shore. These burdens were carried in crates or panniers. ' The little creatures do wonders ; they set out at break of day and never halt until the work of the day is finished, going forty-eight miles,' says Mr. Gilchrist."

Another reference is made to the ponies of Sutherlandshire by Captain J. Henderson who, in his book *A General View of the Agriculture of Sutherlandshire* (published in 1812), says :—

" Upon the extensive farms of the east coast of Sutherlandshire there are large horses kept for the plough and cart, but in the other parts of the district the native breed of ' garrons ' are used for the plough, four abreast and in some cases three abreast. Four of these garrons are generally kept to plough 8 to 10 acres of arable land. Their food is the pasture of the fields and moors summer and winter, except that in severe weather they are kept in stables or sheds when they are fed with straw, and that during the spring labour they get some meadow hay. Their price is from four to ten guineas, according to size and quality. They are from eleven hands to thirteen hands high. Their colours are black, brown and grey."

PONIES FOR THE LOVAT SCOUTS.

In 1904 and 1905, when the late Lord Lovat raised the Lovat Scouts after the South African War, I saw the ponies from West Sutherland and Ross-shire tied in the lines near Beaufort Castle where the annual training took place. Among them were many typical strong ponies, the majority of which were dun or dark cream in colour. Compared with the Skye and Uist ponies in the lines near by, I thought they were of a better class.

CLYDESDALE BLOOD.

At one time Caithness bred many Highland ponies which were bought as yearlings by dealers who sold them in Orkney. The invasion of the Clydesdale then took place, and although the famous sire " Glenbruar " was purchased in 1905 by the Duke of Portland for the use of the tenants on his Berriedale estate, he was sparingly taken advantage of and only became famous in later life (p. 103).

It is of interest to note here that much the same happened to one of the most famous Clydesdale sires, " Baron's Pride," who, when he travelled the New Monkland district of Lanarkshire as a three-year-old, was very little taken advantage of. Eventually he was bought by Mr. Montgomerie for £70 and became one of the finest Clydesdale stallions on record.

Since the increase in the number of smallholdings in Caithness many of the crofters have found the large, modern bred Clydesdale too difficult to keep, and in recent years they have been making extensive use of the Highland pony stallions provided by the Department of Agriculture for Scotland. The crofters find that those pony sires cross well with their Clydesdale mares, and leave strong sturdy garrons which can do the work of the holdings just as well as can the big Clydesdales, and which can be fed at about half the cost.

CHAPTER V.

GAICK PONIES.

THE late Mr. William Mackenzie on the Gaick Forest about 1833 bought some of the best of the Corriechuille stud and brought them east into the Badenoch country. The most noted of this strain was " Gaick Callaig." This grand old type of a Lochaber pony when sixteen years old and carrying her ninth foal was secured by Lord Arthur Cecil for £64 and passed into the New Forest. At the same time her own son was sold for £75 to the Congested Districts Board, and forwarded to Professor Cossar Ewart's experimental station at Penicuik where he was named " Atholl." This sire was got by " Herd Laddie " and owned later by the D.O.A.S., where he did good service by siring some of the Department's most useful sires, including among them the Skye bred stallion " Macpherson," referred to when dealing with the Beechwood Stud.

CHAPTER VI.

GLENORCHY PONIES.

GLENORCHY was for a long period of time a great centre of pony breeding. Writing of the great snowstorm of 1554, the chronicler of Finlarig, the ancient monastic institution on the side of Loch Tay, says :—

" There was no thaw till 17th January. It was the greatest snowstorm that was seen in the memory of man living. Many little wild horses and mares, kye, sheep and goats perished and died for want of food in the mountains and other parts."

These " little wild horses " were no doubt the ponies indigenous to the district.

Shortly after this period, if not before, attempts were made to improve the breed, as is shown by the following letter from Lord David Murray, then Private Secretary to James VI. of Scotland and I. of England :—

" To the Right Honourable the Laird of Glenorquhay.

Honourable Sir :—The Prince received a pair of eagles very thankfullie and we hade good sport with thame and according to his promise he hath sent you a horse to be a stallion, one of the best in his stable for that purpose and comendis him kyndlie to you and says that seven years hence when he comes to Scotland he hopes to gett some of his breed. You shall excuse that he was so long in coming for this is

the first that he gave away since the time that ye was
here and you know that I will be ever ready to serve
you or to do you any pleasure that lyes in my power
without any ceremonie and therefore I will not use
any faire words with you for that is needless among
frendis, but remember that I am a true Scotsman,
unchangeable for all I can see here, and I think so
to continue by God's Grace to my lyve's end.   Thus
recommending you to the protection of God, I rest
ever your loving friend to do you service,

D. MURRAY.

Whitehall, 9th January, 1609."

The Royal mews then contained many varieties
of horses—Spanish, Arab, Turkish, etc.—all of them
considered superior to the native Scottish breed in
pace, style, and symmetry.

Though a great deal of good was no doubt done
by Royal patronage of the kind indicated in the above
letter, private enterprise was not lacking.   Thus,
writing of the Thanes of Cawdor in his book, *Scotland
During the Middle Ages,* Cosmo Innes says :—" Somewhat more care is shown of the breed of horses.
Long before this time the lairds of Glenorchy had
introduced English and foreign horses for their great
stud in Perthshire, and the example was followed in
Cawdor."

The reputation of the Glenorchy Stud, there is
every reason to believe, extended to various parts of
the mainland and to the Islands, and no doubt much
of the character of the Highland pony came from that
great horse-breeding preserve.   In Glenorchy everything seems to have been carried out in the most
systematic manner possible, and probably someone

had gone South to study the practical working of the various enactments made in England regarding the castration of all those colts which did not attain to certain standards of height. More than a century later, the same careful system of management still prevailed, as is shown by the following extract from *The Black Book of Taymouth* :—

" John, Earl of Breadalbane, lets to John McNab for five years the grazing hills of Bentechie and Elraig with the full accustomed places where his Lordship's and his predecessors' horses were wont to pasture in Glenorchy, delivering to him thirty stud mares either with foal or having foals at their feet, the one half worth thirty merks apiece, as also 100 merks Scots to buy a sufficient stallion not exceeding five years of age to be kept with the mares on the said grass, and the said John McNab is to keep the mares and stallion on his own peril and to be answerable for them in all cases, excepting only the cases of daylight depredations and public harrying in a hostile manner and to be keep the stallion from labour. To pay the Earl the sum of ten pounds Scots for each of the lands yearly in name of tack duty and at the expiry of his tack to redeliver to the Earl the same number of mares and foals and a stallion of equal value to these he received, or to pay the foresaid prices for the mares and the stallions that are awanting. And in like manner ten pounds for every foal that shall be short of the number of thirty as above mentioned, delivering also the Earl's burning irons which he received for marking the horses.

" *Finlarig,* 11*th June,* 1702."

CHAPTER VII.

CORRIECHUILLE AND HIS STUD.

SOME time previous to 1833, John Cameron of Corriechuille in Lochaber owned a noted stud of Highland ponies. They were of all colours—greys, duns, yellow creams, and piebalds. " Corrie," the name by which Mr. Cameron was usually known, was in his day one of the most extensive farmers and dealers of whom we have record. His dealing career started when, as a boy, he purchased a goat which he sold at a good profit. From that time he steadily advanced, and it is said that eventually he used to present for sale at the September Falkirk Tryst as many as 2,000 Highland cattle and 20,000 sheep.

THE TREK TO THE TRYST.

To give an idea of the scale on which " Corrie " farmed, it may be noted that the cattle which he bought in Skye, after crossing the ferry at Kylerhea to the mainland near Balmacarra, rested each night on their road journey to Falkirk Tryst on one of his own farms. The rate of travel for cattle was about fifteen miles per day, and this gives some indication of the number of farms held by him. He not only rented land on this route, but in many other parts of Scotland, as well as in England.

A native of Carron Water in Stirlingshire, who is now well over eighty years of age, told me that his father remembered when " Corrie's " herds and flocks used to pass along Carron Water road on their way to Falkirk. His numerous droves covered the road for over five miles. " Corrie " himself always rode a piebald Highland pony and constantly went round his flocks and herds. There probably was not a better known agriculturist in the whole of Britain.

" Corrie " is said to have been possessed of a tremendous energy, and the distances he is reputed to have covered on his piebald mare in comparatively short time, seem almost incredible.

THANKS WHERE DUE.

On one occasion " Corrie," along with his shepherds, was hunting wild goats on the banks of the Spean in Lochaber. This river flows very swiftly when it is in flood, as it happened to be that day, and while " Corrie " was hurriedly scrambling along the steep banks, he stumbled and fell headlong into the water. He was being quickly carried down stream when he grasped an overhanging hazel bush and struggled to safety on the bank. One of the shepherds, a devout Lochaber Roman Catholic, was much relieved at his master's safe delivery and addressed him saying,

" Now, ' Corrie,' since God has safely delivered you from drowning, I think you should go down on your knees and offer Him up thanks for doing so."

To this " Corrie " quickly replied,

" That is all very well, Donald, but even He must confess that I was not slack myself."

THE INFLUENCE OF " CORRIE'S " STUD.

The Corriechuille stud formed the foundation of the noted Gaick stud in Badenoch, and the famous mare, " Gaick Callaig," foaled in 1886, had a splatch of white which was a distinct trace of the blood of " Corrie's " piebald mare. At that time Mr. Aeneas Macdonnell of Morar had also a strain of piebalds which was said to have been descended from the Corriechuille strain.

CHAPTER VIII.

THE DRUMCHORRY STUD.

THE Drumchorry stud of Highland ponies, which belonged to the late Mr. Donald Stewart, took a prominent place in the show ring at the Highland and Agricultural Society's shows in the closing years of the last and the opening years of the present century. Before he removed to Drumchorry, Mr. Stewart had his stud at Glenloy, six miles from Achnacarry, and it was the only stud of note in that district since the time of Corriechuille (see p. 100). In it was conserved a good deal of the old blood which has been found so useful at Gaick (see p. 96). At one time or another Mr. Stewart drew from all good, pure strains, including that of Atholl through " Glengarry " and " Herd Laddie," and that of North Uist through the two sires " Heather " and " Mosscrop " (see p. 41).

The Drumchorry mares were handed down from father to son for many generations, but it is generally thought that they originally came out of the Kirkmichael district where many of the old-fashioned gig-pony Clydesdale greys referred to by Mr. Dykes (p. 121) were to be found.

Although Mr. Stewart of Drumchorry was not the breeder of the famous sire, " Glenbruar " (see p. 105), he must be given the credit of discovering him and showing him as a three-year-old at the

Glasgow Highland and Agricultural Show in 1905, when he was first in his class and won the silver medal given by the Polo and Riding Pony Society. He was bred by the late James Macdonald of Ruidhchlachrie, Blair Atholl, and was sired by "Herd Laddie," who brought fame to the Atholl stud (p. 81).

At this 1905 show Mr. Stewart sold "Glenbruar" to Mr. Turner, Commissioner for His Grace the Duke of Portland, who sent him to the Duke's estate of Berridale in Caithness for the use of the crofters.

When I was judging the Highland ponies at the Inverness Highland and Agricultural Society Show in 1932, the Duke of Portland watched the proceedings with interest and then sent his factor at Berridale, Mr. George King, to tell me that he would like to speak to me. I was duly presented to His Grace, and he informed me that he once owned "Glenbruar" and that he had been surprised to learn from the Show catalogue that most of the Highland ponies shown that day were descended from him. I expressed the opinion that they could not have better blood than "Glenbruar's," and the Duke turned to Mr. King and asked, "Why did we sell 'Glenbruar,' Mr. King?" The answer was that the crofters thought him too small and would not use him. (See p. 103).

After remaining at Berridale for three years, "Glenbruar" was sold to Major Logan of Inverness who drove him in a light two-wheeled buggy. I can recall seeing him being driven through the streets of Inverness by Major Logan and being impressed by the freedom with which he moved and by the elegance of his carriage.

CHAPTER IX.

ROSEHAUGH STUD AND "JOCK," KING GEORGE V.'S PONY.

MAJOR LOGAN (p. 103) sold "Glenbruar" to the late Mr. James Douglas Fletcher of Rosehaugh, who used him in his stud with much success, although unfortunately all his colts were gelded. Through the prepotency of "Glenbruar" this stud, in the hands of Mrs. Shaw-MacKenzie, rose to considerable fame in the showyards during the years succeeding the Great War, and the female stock got by "Glenbruar" includes "Lady Phœnix" who won two Highland and Agricultural Society championships, including the gold medal at the centenary show at Edinburgh. Another mare, "Lady Kilcoy," won the championship at Aberdeen in 1928, and the stud has had many other successes, too numerous to mention, with animals of "Glenbruar" blood.

Not only has the Rosehaugh stud had a noted showyard career, but it is also famed for having bred the best-known Highland pony in the world—the late King George the Fifth's "Jock." This pony, which was King George's favourite, was bred by Mr. Douglas Fletcher and foaled at Rosehaugh in 1921. He was sold to Donald Scott, a small farmer, and by him to Major Logan of Inverness, from whom he was bought for King George by Sir Arthur Erskine, the Crown Equerry.

Sir Arthur writes me that "the King took him to Balmoral and to Sandringham and never rode any

H

other pony when he was out shooting. He was a perfect pony in every way—not too fast and not too slow, had a perfect mouth and a comfortable trot. In fact, it was absurd to see the pony walking about after the King like a dog, thanks perhaps to the carrots which were always being produced for his benefit by the King. Needless to say, the pony was always marvellously turned out by his groom, French, his flowing snow-white mane and long tail specially catching the eye."

As I have already said, " Jock " is the best-known Highland pony in the world ; King George's last outings at Sandringham were taken on his faithful back, and few of us who saw the film of the Royal funeral procession will ever forget the pathos of the riderless pony.

For the sake of the breed, it is most unfortunate that " Jock " was gelded (all the more unfortunate as I have been told that it was almost decided to keep him entire), for he is a beautiful and typical animal of the breed. His dam was " Lady Strathnairn " and his sire the noted " Glenbruar " (see p. 103), whose sire was " Herd Laddie," who brought fame to the Atholl stud in the early eighties (p. 82). The sire of " Herd Laddie " was " Highland Laddie," bred in Lochaber, and his sire was " Macneil's Canna," who, as has already been related (p. 56) was bred in the Island of Mull and sired by a grey horse bred by Mr. Campbell of Ulva. This grey horse was sired by a brown entire which belonged to the Duke of Argyll's factor in Mull and which had been brought from America in a sailing ship by the factor's brother who was a sea captain (p. 56).

"LADY KILCOY"

CHAPTER X.

TWO PERTHSHIRE STUDS—DUNIRA AND ELCHO PARK.

THE Dunira stud was established in Perthshire In it have been used several sires bred by Mr. Mackelvie of Arran (p. 63), and through them " Glenbruar " blood has been introduced. This stud has shown successfully at Highland and Agricultural Society's shows ; one of their best mares, " White Spot," a beautiful grey got by " Mountain Ranger," a Fell pony, was first as a filly in 1928, and first as a mare at Melrose in 1936, and the stud contains several other winners.

ELCHO PARK STUD.

Elcho Park stud, near Perth, is the property of Major Moncrieff Wright and contains many typical Highland ponies, several of which have won honours at Highland and Agricultural Society's shows. The best mare in the stud is " Staffin Princess " which won the championship of the breed at Melrose in 1936. She was bred in Skye, her sire being " Failie Will Power," a son of " May Dew," which founded the Beechwood stud of the Department of Agriculture for Scotland (p. 113). This animal is probably the best mare of the breed now alive, and I doubt if anyone can recall a better. A daughter of a mare

bred by the late King George V. is also in this stud—
her mother won two championships at Highland and
Agricultural Society's Shows.

" Macpherson " and " Glenbernesdale " are the
two stud sires. The former was bred in Skye and
was previously used successfully at Beechwood, while
the latter was also bred in Skye and sired by " Glenbruar "—he was twice champion at the Highland
and Agricultural Society's shows, and, though now
twenty-two years of age, still looks young.

Major Moncrieff Wright tried an interesting
experiment in the 1936 season. He served one of his
Highland pony mares with a Percheron stallion
which was travelling in Perthshire. His object was
to put more size into his stud, and in this he was
only repeating what was done in the Atholl stud in
the time of King James IV.

"ISLE OF ARRAN, BONNIE JEAN"

Bred by King George V.

CHAPTER XI.

BEECHWOOD STUD.

THIS stud was started when the Congested Districts Board, in its early days, entrusted to Professor Cossar Ewart the task of making experiments to find pony stallions for the crofters which would be more suitable for their mares than those then in use. The Professor was also instructed to take into account hardiness, cost of upkeep, utility on the land, suitability for hill work or for service with mounted infantry, and eventual marketing at a profit, while it was expressly stated that Clydesdales and their crosses were barred.

These experiments were carried on for a few years at The Bungalow, Penicuik, Midlothian, and the Professor bought ponies from Connemara, Iceland, Norway, as well as from Uist, Barra, and Skye. On those mares he used Arab, English thoroughbred, and Highland pony sires.

When the Congested Districts Board bought the estate of Kilmuir in Skye, the Professor's assorted stud was moved to the farm of Monkstadt on that estate. At that time I was tenant of the farm of Duntulm near Monkstadt, and I had thus every opportunity of watching this interesting but hopeless experiment, and of foretelling its ultimate fate. My prophecies were fulfilled when Mr. William Barbour, a gentleman with a wide knowledge of agricultural

conditions in Scotland, became a member of the
Board of Agriculture for Scotland, and was given
entire charge of its live-stock breeding operations.
As he was a practical stocksman, he soon saw the
folly of the methods followed by Professor Ewart,
and within a short time he had disposed of most of
the different types of pony which he knew would be
of no help in improving the breed, and retained only
a few strong native ponies.

Two of the best of the ponies kept by Mr.
Barbour were " Atholl," a grey entire of good size
and substance which was bred at Gaick and got by
" Herd Laddie " (p. 81), and a beautiful grey mare
presented to the Congested Districts Board by Sir
John Gilmour, Bart., of Montrave. I remember this
grey mare—she was descended from " Herd Laddie "
and was the best type of garron then in the country.
Strangely enough, she was of the type that the best
breeders of the present day are striving to produce.
When this fine mare was at Penicuik, Professor Ewart
served her with all sorts of sires, and as a result a
good part of her valuable breeding time was wasted.
After the removal to Monkstadt, however, Mr.
Barbour served her with a sire called " Braemore,"
and she gave birth to the noted sire " Hebridean "
which has made an excellent and lasting impression
on the breed.

At that time good and typical Highland pony
sires were difficult to procure, for there were very few
in the country, but the Congested Districts Board
managed to get two in addition to " Atholl." These
were " Roderick " and " Braemore." " Roderick,"
who was bred in Lochbroom, was dark brown in

colour and, although under the size wanted at the present day, was a pony of great thickness and was typical of his breed. He travelled Skye and other districts, and when owned by the late Mr. Munro of Lemlair, Dingwall, won first prize at one of the Highland and Agricultural Society's shows. " Braemore " was bred by the late Mr. McHardy, Braemore, Lochbroom, and was much the same size as " Roderick," though he was not of such a good type. He was of a dark cream colour with eel stripe, had a great flow of tail, and had a profuse mane and forelock which helped to conceal a rather large head.

When the Congested Districts Board was replaced by the Board of Agriculture for Scotland, the stock-breeding activities increased considerably under the supervision of the late Mr. James Wood and later of Mr. Frank Thomson. Eventually the Board rented the fertile farm of Beechwood and two or three high-lying farms in the vicinity of Inverness, and to them were removed the Highland pony stud and the pedigree herd of Highland cattle.

A VISIT TO BEECHWOOD.

In the spring of 1936 I was privileged to inspect the stock on those farms, and I was much impressed not only by the high standard of management, but also by the superior quality of the animals. Although my main purpose was to see the stud of Highland ponies, my interest in the other live-stock was soon aroused, and a short account of the other activities at Beechwood may not be out of place.

The Department of Agriculture for Scotland owns a small but select fold of Highland cattle which it was prompted to start because of the long-established and continual decrease in the number of folds in the country. Of recent years, however, the demand for Highland bulls from crofters in the West has decreased considerably, and the demand for Shorthorn and Aberdeen Angus bulls has risen in proportion; the crofters have found that by crossing those bulls with Highland cows they get animals which command a much more profitable market than do the pure-bred Highland cattle. Those of us who are familiar with conditions in the Western Islands often ask ourselves what is going to be the end of all this " crossing." The answer is that the crofter will ultimately find himself with a breed of cattle which his land cannot support, and that he will then be forced to go back to the native Highland breed.

This is the position which the Department of Agriculture for Scotland, in its wisdom, has foreseen, and against which it has safeguarded by establishing at Beechwood a fold of Highland cattle to which the crofter can turn for supplies when he needs them. Although the fold is small, it is very select, and it is kept under natural conditions, all the stock being wintered out of doors and never under a roof. The male calves are kept as bulls, and while some of the heifers are used to maintain the fold, the balance are sold for breeding purposes. It seems to me that the time is now ripe for increasing the fold, since it cannot be long till more crofters in the West are forced to apply for Highland bulls.

An interesting sight which I witnessed at Beech-

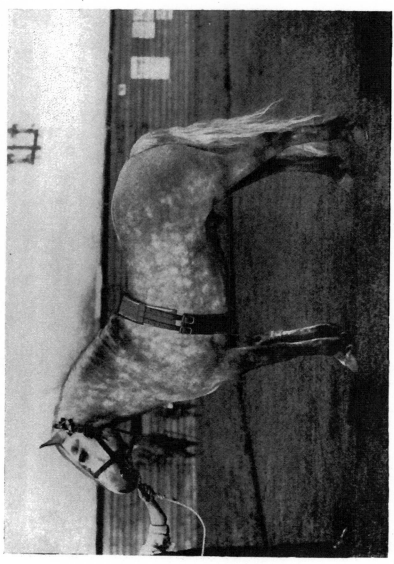

Photo. "FAILLIE ROVER" Brown

wood, and one which could not be seen anywhere else in Scotland, was a lot of 400 blackfaced rams. They were being removed to a change of pasture, and as they passed along the farm road I had a good opportunity of viewing them at close quarters. This large flock of rams is replenished each season by purchases at the annual ram sales. The animals are kept on the Department's farms, except when they are let out to crofters for use at a nominal fee. After its third season in use a ram is sold—and nothing testifies more to the high standard of the flock than the fact that, even at this age, the rams are bought by sheep-farmers who wish to improve their stock.

THE BEECHWOOD STUD.

The Beechwood stud has been bred practically from one mare, " May Dew," a daughter of the famous " Glenbruar " (p. 104). She was bred by me, and won second prize at Paisley Show of the Highland and Agricultural Society in 1913. That same year she went to the Beechwood stud, and though she is now twenty-six years of age, she still breeds regularly every year. At the present time there are nineteen of her descendants in the stud, including six of her sons which are used as stallions and one of which, " Failie Diamond," was first at the 1931 show of the Highland and Agricultural Society. Her daughter, " May Dew II.," was also a first prize winner at the same show.

" May Mist," a full sister of " May Dew," was bred by Mr. Thomson of Castleton, Avoch, and won first prize when I showed her at the Cupar

Show of the Highland and Agricultural Society. She
also joined the Beechwood stud, and when shown from
there won the championship at one of the Highland
shows. Although she is a better looking mare than
her sister " May Dew," she has never come up to
the same high standard of consistent breeding, but
she has to her credit in the Beechwood stud " Failie
Rover," first prize winner and champion at the 1927
show of the Highland and Agricultural Society.

The prevailing colour of the Beechwood stud
is grey, but there are a few duns. The type of pony
that has been arrived at is typical of the breed.
Some increase in size might be considered necessary
for the present needs of the crofters and smallholders,
but the difficulty is to procure outside blood of the
necessary size and quality. I have dealt with this
difficulty in Chapter XII.

The entire stud numbers well over thirty, and
there are nine stallions which travel various districts.

Of late years the sire that has been most success-
fully used in the stud is a black stallion named
" MacPherson," bred in Skye and sired by " Atholl "
The sire in use at the present time is " Fender
Laddie," which was sired by " Bonnie Laddie "
(p. 81) and bred in the Atholl stud.

The dam of those two noted mares, " May Mist "
and " May Dew," was bred near Bonar Bridge in
Sutherlandshire. I also owned her but could not
trace her pedigree, she could have been foaled about
the time the Duke of Sutherland owned " Lord
Reay " and probably would have been sired by him.
She was a strong-built mare, cream-coloured with the
usual black eel stripe, a rather large white blaze on

"MAY DEW" AND HER PROGENY

"Knocknagael Prince"   "Knocknagael Chief"   "Knocknagael Monarch"
"Faillie Diamond"   "Faillie Gay Boy"   "Faillie Comet"   "May Dew"

face and two white (well up to the hocks) hind legs. Those markings showed distinct traces of Clydesdale blood of which I would say she would have one third. She was lifted during the war for war purposes.

CHAPTER XII.

THE GENERAL CHARACTERISTICS OF THE HIGHLAND PONIES : SOME SUGGESTIONS FOR THE IMPROVEMENT OF THE BREED.

DIFFERENT TYPES OF PONY.

ALL Highland ponies are descended from common ancestors, but they have been differentiated into separate types, each with certain characteristics of its own. The differentiation may be attributed to four main causes : firstly to environment, secondly to their treatment by man, thirdly to selection for particular kinds of work, and fourthly to the attempts made at different times to improve the breeds by the introduction of crosses of more or less alien strains of blood.

Apart from the characteristics impressed upon the breed by environment and by the various purposes for which the ponies are kept, the most valuable qualities possessed by Highland ponies are their sturdy constitution, their keen intelligence, and their concentrated vitality, all of which are common to the entire breed.

Owing to the large increase of smallholders all over Scotland, the demand for the strong, stout, and good-sized Highland pony is increasing at the present day. Unfortunately, most of the smallholders and hill farmers in the South know practically nothing of the Highland pony, and have to use a larger and softer breed which is economically ill-adapted to do their work. A Highland garron on such a holding would be an asset which has only to be experienced to be fully appreciated. Also, the cost of the upkeep of a stout Highland garron would be but half that of many of the animals at present employed, and it would do the work as well, if not better.

THE COLOURS OF HIGHLAND PONIES.

The colour of Highland ponies varies pretty much the same as in other breeds of horses, but the most favoured colour is dun and dark cream, with a black eel stripe along the back and dark points. White markings are not common, though a small star on the forehead and one white hind hoof are not considered to be blemishes.

The commonest colour of all is grey, and this can be accounted for by the prepotency of "Herd Laddie" (see p. 81), and his impressive son, "Glenbruar" (see p. 104). Although this colour is true to the breed, most breeders would prefer the darker shades, and for deer forest ponies it is definitely considered to be a disadvantage. Dun and dark cream, black, brown, and dark bay are quite good colours, while chestnuts with light-coloured mane and tail are fairly prevalent among Uist ponies (these having been increased by the use of a Norwegian sire of that colour which was imported into South Uist. Strawberry roans are not numerous, but they are not objected to. Skewbalds have not been known, and although Corriechuille had a famous strain of piebalds, it has

now died out. In any case, the Stud Book rules
recognise neither skewbald nor piebald.

POINTS OF A GOOD PONY.

The general symmetry of all good horses is
much the same, and the Highland pony is no exception.
It is important that he should be deep through the
heart, short and strong in the back, well-ribbed up,
and sprung and deep in the barrel. The shoulders
should be long and well sloped, tapering to distinct
withers. The quarters should be broad and long,
with tail well set up.

Many of our Highland ponies are often short
and straight in the shoulders and lacking in withers.
This kind of shoulder is possibly more common
among the heavier or garron ponies, although the
lighter type is by no means free from it. Some of
the old-fashioned breeders thought this heavy, coarse
shoulder a sign of strength, and, because of this idea,
no steps were taken by breeders to avoid it. It has
to be admitted, however, that there are few, if any,
more discomforting feelings than to find oneself,
when riding over rough ground, seated on a saddle that
has slipped on to the pony's neck. A Highland
pony should have the height of wither necessary to
keep a properly girthed saddle in its right position
no matter how rough and steep the ground may be.
Indeed, the same applies to horses of every breed,
and the best working Clydesdales that ever I owned
had, without exception, high-set withers and long
sloping shoulders.

The neck of a Highland pony should be of

medium length, well arched and powerful, fine at the gullet, and carrying the head high and well forward.

The head should be small and short, wide across the forehead, relatively long from ear to eye, with a square muzzle and wide, open nostrils. The eyes should be large, full, and prominent, and there should be a slight hollow, or " dish," immediately below them. The eyes should also be looking well forward so that they can be clearly seen from the front. The ears should be wide set and erect, not too big, and pointing well forward.

The limbs should be strong and muscular, with long and powerful fore-arms and thighs, while the knees and hocks should be large and low-set, with plenty of clean flat bone below them, and the pasterns should be of medium length. The feet should be large, round, open, and of fairly hard and thoroughly sound texture.

The necessity that a Highland pony should be a good and fast walker cannot but be appreciated when it is realised that most of his daily work has to be done at this gait. Those of us who have followed a sturdy Highland pony carrying a fifteen-stone stag out of a deep corrie along gravelly scree and through treacherous bogs, and who have watched how it swings its tail at every step as a well-proportioned man swings his kilt, keeping up a steady four miles an hour, fully appreciate how important it is to put the greatest value on a pony that can walk well. The action should be true and straight, for dishing, straddling, and wide hock movement are glaring faults. Knees, pasterns, and hocks should be freely and powerfully flexed, without any tendency to the rounded action of the hackney.

The Highland pony has the great advantage of an amazing longevity, and there are many accredited instances of ponies living to the age of thirty-five and upwards. Among the stud-book ponies, the noted " Glenbruar " died at twenty-six, and I remember that his sire, " Herd Laddie," was shown at a Highland Show when he was that age, and looked as if he was good for another ten years.

The Highland pony is almost entirely free from any disease of the nervous system—I have never come across a shiverer, and very seldom have I seen an animal suffering from stringhalt. Bone disease, which is sometimes noticeable in Uist and other Outer Hebridean islands, is a result of putting the animals to heavy work when they are too young. Highland ponies are said to be free from grass sickness.

There should be a tuft of straight hair at the heels, and the body should be covered with an outer coat of strong, badger hair with a soft, short and close undercoat—both coats giving ample warmth and protection against the cold and wet climatic conditions that the ponies have to endure. The hair on the mane and tail should grow thickly and should be long and of a strong fibre, while many of the old-fashioned garrons showed a distinct wave in the fibre.

THE HEIGHT OF HIGHLAND PONIES.

The height of Highland ponies is limited to 14.2 hands. Owing to the increase in the number of small-holdings, however, many of which are now placed on some of the best land in the country, and to the great changes in economic conditions, the call for an increase in size is urgent, not only for the welfare of the small-holder, but also for the good of the breed. This is a subject which I have mentioned several times, and it was this urgency for increase in size that, more than anything, led me to write this book.

The Highland ponies of the earlier periods were, as I have already shown, from 11 to 13 hands in height, and at that size they seem to have been well adapted for what little work they had to do. As time went on, the need for heavier ponies became more insistent and led to crossing with larger sires. In this book I have traced the different breeds of sire that have been used for this purpose during the last fifty years or so, especially in the Islands (which, after all, are the home of the breed), and I think I have proved that the most suitable of all is the Clydesdale. In this connection there is considerable interest attached to the following note by Mr. Thomas Dykes in his article on Highland Ponies in *The Transactions of the Highland and Agricultural Society for* 1905 :—

" Up to forty years ago, grey mares of ancient and undiluted Clydesdale type were commonly to be found stabled in all the country inns in Kilmarnock and Ayr on market days—hardy, useful short-legged sorts which might still have been preserved but for the fact that there were no stallions of their size and activity and type available. Some of these old-fashioned gig pony Clydesdale greys found their way into the North, and no doubt had much to do with forming the modern types of mainland ponies.

I

It is not strictly speaking ' pony ' blood, but it was brought there when it was wanted, has done much good, and may do a lot of good yet if properly mated."

INCREASING THE SIZE OF THE PONIES.

For nearly thirty years the Department of Agriculture for Scotland has been supplying Highland pony sires for the use of the crofters, and every credit is due to it for having helped to fix a type. Now, however, that crofters have been settled on much of the best grazing and arable land, there is an urgent need for a heavier type of pony, and, from information I have received from different parts of the country, I have come to the conclusion that, although the sires supplied by the Department have in the past served a most useful purpose, many of them are now too small for modern requirements.

The problem then is to find how to increase the size of the ponies with the least possible delay, and at the same time to maintain the characteristic hardiness of the breed. The most direct and safest solution would without doubt be obtained by a judicious introduction of Clydesdale blood. Two methods of doing this suggest themselves, and in both there would have to be very careful selection of both sires and mares.

The first method that I suggest is that a few of the present stud of Highland pony mares in the hands of the Department of Agriculture for Scotland should be mated to a carefully chosen Clydesdale sire. The fillies bred in this manner should be mated in turn to a good Highland pony stallion, and the colts bred out of those fillies should be kept entire and sent out for the use of the crofters.

The other method would be to mate a selected Highland sire to selected Clydesdale mares, to mate the fillies bred in this manner to a Highland pony stallion, and to use the colts bred out of these fillies as already suggested.

Both those methods of introducing Clydesdale blood have been done in the past, though in a very haphazard manner, but their value has been amply proved by the breeding record of "Islesman," "Moss Crop," and "Rory o' the Hills," as well as the dam of the two famous mares, "May Mist" and "May Dew," at Beechwood, all of whom I mentioned when dealing with the ponies of Skye and Uist. I feel certain that with proper care and selection they could now be used with even more satisfactory results.

The urgency of the crofters' need for ponies of an increased size has placed the breed in a perilous position, for I understand that at the present time the crofters, especially those in the Islands, are making use of several inferior sires with little, if anything, to commend them but their size. The crofters have long realised that the value of a pony increases almost in direct proportion to inches of height at the withers, but the extra inches gained by use of the poor stallions referred to are proving the most direct way to destroy the good work done by the Department of Agriculture for Scotland during the last thirty years. The situation, then, is serious, but it can be rectified if, without delay, the Department will place at the disposal of the crofters sires bred in the manner I have described.

Those sires would be of the size that is now wanted, and as all the animals used in their breeding would be selected with extreme care, they would still maintain the hardy characteristics of the native breed.

PART III.

REMINISCENCES.

Some random reminiscences of Ponies and Men, and of Life in Skye in the days now almost forgotten.

CHAPTER I.

SHEEP HANDLING—THE COAL BARQUE— THE DEVIL IN THE GLEN—SWEARING.

A HELPING HAND TO THE NEIGHBOURS.

At all the most important yearly happenings on the farm—those, at least, which were important to me when I was a boy, such as sheep-shearing, peat-cutting and the marking of the " dash," the neighbouring crofters gave a .helping hand. As a rule the local schoolmaster announced such events to his pupils a few days beforehand, and they carried home the news to their parents who turned up to a man to do their bit. The cordial spirit which existed between them and *fear-a-baile* (to-day he would be called " the boss ") now seems to me to be too good to be true.

At all those jobs the helpers were fed liberally with the plain, but substantial fare then in vogue, and refreshed by copious draughts from the wicker-clad grey-beard—though never to excess. *Fear-a-baile*, although himself a non-smoker, procured with his annual grocery order a roll of black twist or bogie roll tobacco, ten or twelve pounds in weight. On such days as I have mentioned, his bulging pocket contained a large ball of this tobacco. As he talked and joked with the elder members of his willing helpers he usually ended by producing the ball and handing a good length of it to the man with whom he was speaking. The bond of friendship that existed between him and those men may hardly seem credible in this modern age of commercialism—they trusted and respected him, and whenever they were in want he helped them, just as readily as they helped him when he had need of them.

Although *fear-a-baile* took a practical interest in everything about the farm, he left the management of the arable land to Iain Bhan, his faithful grieve. But when it came to the handling of the sheep, he himself was undoubtedly the " boss." The invitation to the crofters to come and help at peat-cutting, hay-making, etc., was what may be termed a public invitation, but when it came to sheep handlings, it was only men who were thoroughly used to sheep who were asked. I was often sent round on my dun coloured Highland pony with a list of the men I was to invite. This list always contained a few reserve names, in case some of the good men were unable to come.

CLIPPINGS.

Sheep shearing was the most important handling, and in some seasons, owing to the excessive rainfall, it was very much delayed. There is no job on a farm which can be so upset by rain, especially if it begins when the open-air clipping of milk ewes is in full swing, for then all operations have to be suspended. When this happened, the clippers would wile away the time of waiting for the sheep to dry by engaging in athletic sports. All forms of athletics were indulged in, and most of the men were very skilful, but at hop, step and leap none could beat the " pin-leg tailor." He stotted off his pin-leg in an extraordinary manner, and when he took the final leap the leg was forced deeply into the ground.

At those clippings, each man had his own earth stool year after year, and in some cases generation after generation. Much the same applied to certain jobs such as buisting, crogging, and wool-binding and packing, which were always done by the same men, each of whom was an expert in his own line.

When I returned from school on a clipping day, I had a hurried meal and then made straight for the fanks. *Fear-a-baile* had always a job waiting for me—as a rule it consisted of picking up the broken wool round the clipping stools. During any short absence of *fear-a-baile*, however, I usually entertained myself by such aesthetic pursuits as seeing how high in the air I could squirt the milk from the teats of the ewes as they lay on their backs on the clipping stools—sometimes my target was the flowing beard of one or other of the shearers.

As I grew older I was entrusted with the buisting —the stamping of the tar brand on each clipped sheep. This was the job about which *fear-a-baile* was most particular. I had to hold my buisting iron at the correct angle and place it on the exact spot of the sheep's anatomy, or else there was trouble. A bad buister advertises himself for a twelve-month, whereas a bad clipper's mistakes vanish in a few weeks.

As I became stronger I was put on to the crogging. This was the catching of the sheep in the bucht and delivering them on to the clipping stools.

It was real hard work, and much discomfort was added to it by the blistering of the hands on the rough horns.

I was next put on to the wool-binding, a job which I hated as it was generally given to a woman. *Fear-a-baile*, however, insisted that I should go through the mill from beginning to end.

The packing of the wool bags was my next task, and as the bag swung from the gallows with me deeply hidden inside, I soon developed something similar to sea-sickness, to which I was prone. This certainly did not add to my comfort or pleasure.

Early one season *fear-a-baile* announced that I was to start clipping, and my elder brother and I took great pains to build the turf stool on which I proudly took my seat in the row of clippers. The expert manner in which the other clippers could handle and clip their sheep was to me at the start rather discouraging, but I soon got the knack.

On the evening of the last day of the clipping, the schoolmaster and a few of *fear-a-baile's* cronies from the village usually turned up at the buchts to see how things were going, and to discover if anything was left in the greybeard.

THE COAL BARQUE.

Another event of importance in our young lives was the arrival each year of the coal boat bringing our supplies. This became a regular event only after the drift to the towns of the younger generation had begun and labour had become less plentiful. Also, farmers began to grow more turnips, and as the work on this crop clashed with peat-cutting, *fear-a-baile* came to the conclusion that it would be cheaper to buy coal. Good coal in those days could be delivered on the beach below our house for twelve shillings, and never more than fifteen shillings, a ton.

The arrival of the two-masted schooner early in June each year, was eagerly watched for, and I can still see it coming up the loch, often in a dead calm, when it was towed by the ship's dinghy with four of the crew at the oars. It was brought as far up the sandy beach as possible at high water, and the ebbing tide left it high and dry, lying on its side. The cargo was not all for *fear-a-baile*, and generally it was shared with the clergymen, the schoolmaster, and the doctor.

THE SKIPPER.

The same ship came year after year, and the old skipper, who was also the owner, was a real old sea-dog. He had sailed all over the world in his young days, and he used to relate his adventures to *fear-a-baile*, while I eagerly listened and marvelled at his tales of hair-breadth escapes and awful hardships when going round " the Horn."

After he had made enough money to buy the old barque, the skipper said farewell to the Horn and traded in the safer waters round his native island of Arran, with occasional expeditions as far north as Stornoway. He was a worthy of the type of Para Handy, and he had what was then known as a " Paddy shave "—his entire face was clean-shaven with the exception of his chin, on which grew a long tuft of white hair (more often black with coal dust). This gave him the appearance of a billy goat.

As he chalked up each bucket of coal on the shaft of the weighing-beam, the old man often cursed the crofters for their delay in coming forward with their carts to the ship's side. Since his cursing was done in Arran Gaelic, he might as well have been speaking French for all that the Skye men understood, but it was a very different matter when the mate, who was a native of Skye, came to the rescue and translated the captain's remarks into local idiom. The dialects in the Gaelic language vary about as much as they do in English, and the difference between Skye Gaelic and that spoken in Arran, Islay, and some parts of the mainland, is about as great as the difference between the English spoken by an educated native of Inverness town and that spoken by an Aberdeenshire farm-worker. The Gaelic spoken in Skye is generally accepted as being the purest there is.

THE PERFORMING MONKEY.

One incident connected with the arrival of the coal boat may be related here. A gentleman in the Isle of Mull was the owner of a large monkey which his man-servant had taught to perform several clever tricks. When the gentleman died, the servant became the owner of the monkey, and, deciding that he might make a livelihood by travelling round the country with it, he found his way to Tobermory where he intended joining the steamer for the mainland. It so happened that the coal barque, on her way north with our annual supply of coal, had put into Tobermory for provisions, and the skipper offered the monkey and its owner passage to Skye.

When the barque reached our beach, my elder brother, my cousin, and I hurried down to renew old acquaintances. I had never seen a monkey before, except in a picture in one of my nursery books, and the sight of the animal as he walked along the slanting deck both amazed and terrified me.

Now, *fear-a-baile* had a rule that no vagrant or other person in need of a night's lodging was ever to be turned away and that such people were to receive supper, bed, and breakfast. The monkey's owner came under this rule of Highland hospitality, and to show his appreciation, he dressed his animal in its long-tailed black coat and green trousers, and made it do many amusing tricks to the music of the melodeon. After the exhibition was over, the monkey was housed in the harness-room, and the owner retired to the bothy for the night.

AN UNREHEARSED PERFORMANCE.

After we boys had gone to our bedroom, my brother, who was always ready for any mischief, suggested to my cousin and me that we should go and get the monkey out, take him to the back of a knowe and see if we could get him to do his tricks. We were quite agreeable, and in a short time we were on our way through the heather to the knowe, my cousin leading the monkey, and my brother and I following with the melodeon and the dress clothes.

When we arrived at the scene of the performance, we dressed the monkey in his coat and trousers, and my cousin held him by a cord while my brother sat on a stone and played the melodeon. I sat among the heather and watched the proceedings from a safe distance.

The monkey paid no attention to my brother's playing and refused to perform even the simplest of his tricks. A halt was called, and after we had discussed the matter, my cousin blamed my brother for not playing the right tunes. Suddenly, to our amazement, we saw that the monkey had slipped his cord and was making off as hard as he could. My brother, who was pretty fleet of foot, followed closely and was able to catch hold of his tail which protruded through a slit in the coat. The monkey turned to attack him and he was forced to let go. In the gathering dusk of the short June night the monkey was soon out of sight, and there was nothing left for us but to return home and slip into bed as quietly as we could.

THE DEVIL IN THE GLEN.

Next morning being Sunday, people were not early astir, but it was not long before the news spread that the monkey had escaped. My fellow conspirators warned me to keep silent about the doings of the previous evening, and this I faithfully promised to do.

On Monday morning we went to school, and on our way joined the children from one of the neighbouring glens, who told us a long story about the devil having been seen near their home on Saturday night. He had, it appeared, entered one of the cottages through a hole in the thatch, and, dressed in a long-tailed coat and green trousers, he had scared the cottager stiff by dancing on the rafters.

That evening when we were on our way home, we met a local character who went under the name of " Boy-o." He was a navvy by trade, and had at one time worked on the construction of the Mallaig railway. I remember old Hector, the blacksmith, remarking about him one day when he passed the smithy on the way to the local inn.

" There goes the ' Boy-o ' for another drink. That man has drunk as much whisky as would float the steamer *Claymore*."

I am afraid, however, that the pot was calling the kettle black.

Well, we met " Boy-o," and he immediately referred to the devil having been seen in Glen Hinnisdal and asked my brother what he thought about it. As my brother expressed no opinion, the " Boy-o " strongly condemned the rumour as a lie, his reason for this assertion being that four Free Church elders lived in Glen Hinnisdal and that all the inhabitants were holy people who belonged to the Free Church. Because of this, he maintained that the devil would never dream of entering the Glen.

" But," added the ' Boy-o,' " I'll tell you who it is. I just heard yesterday that an Irishman who used to work with me on the Mallaig railway, is on the tramp in Skye. His name is Pat Murphy, and when he got his pay he used to dress himself up in his best Irish style with a black coat and green breeches. He used to carry a short stick and twirl it round his fingers while he sang, ' In Tipperaray I was born.' It will be Pat right enough that was in Glen Hinnisdal."

In due course the monkey was captured in the cliffs above the cottages in the Glen, but the " Boy-o " was so convinced that it was Pat Murphy, that he insisted on going and seeing for himself. On viewing the monkey, he turned round and remarked,

" It's not Pat Murphy, but it is devilish like him after he had been on the spree and had not washed and shaved for a week."

AN EXPERT IN SWEARING.

I have mentioned that the skipper of the coal barque cursed in Gaelic, and this reminds me of an old and much esteemed neighbour of my father's— a man of culture who was descended from a real good old Skye stock. Strange to say, all his forebears for generations back had been famed for swearing. He himself was never known to utter an oath in the English language, but I have heard him swear in the Gaelic with an earnestness of spirit and with a vocabulary which made Iain Ruadh's seem mild (see p. 42).

THE GREAT OATH.

This old gentleman stood on his dignity when in the company of his servants, and would not suffer any swearing among them. On one occasion he and his shepherds were sorting sheep into fanks, the gates of which were not very secure. In due course the sheep were sorted, counted, and placed in different pens, and the men retired behind the fank walls with their master to have some refréshment.

While they were doing so, old Donald the shepherd, who was feeling uneasy about the gates, looked over the wall and saw to his horror that two of them were flat on the ground and that the sheep in the pens were mixing fast. Donald's mind flashed back to the trouble they had already had in sorting the sheep, and he was almost stunned by the prospect of having to begin the day's work over again. He could hardly be blamed if he forgot his master's presence and gave vent to a Gaelic oath of great antiquity and force. When the old gentleman heard Donald's oath, he shouted in a loud voice and reprimanded him for using such language in his presence.

After the sheep had been sorted out again, the master turned to Donald and said with a smile,

" That was a *great* oath you gave out, Donald, when the sheep got mixed."

Donald looked at him and wondered what was coming next.

" Donald," said the old gentleman, " Would you mind repeating it to me ? "

Donald repeated it word for word, but not in the same forceful manner that he had used earlier in the day, for, as he himself remarked, "there was not the same occasion for putting force into it."

The old gentleman then said, " Well, Donald, I thought I knew all the best ones, but as yours is a very good one, and a great favourite of my father's and one that I had forgotten, here is half-a-crown to you for reminding me of it."

CLASS DISTINCTION.

Mention of this old worthy reminds me of a story of him which was related to me by his nephew whom he reproved for swearing in English. In the days

K

when sheep farming was prosperous this old gentleman, like other tacksmen in Skye, always travelled
first class on the railways.   It happened that one year
when he set out for his annual visit to Inverness
Sheep and Wool Fair, the market reports were such
that there was little prospect of getting good prices
for either sheep or wool.   He and a number of other
farmers sailed as usual from Portree to Strome
Ferry which was the terminus before the railway was
extended to Kyle of Lochalsh, and on arriving there
took their places in a first-class compartment.   Shortly
before the train was due to leave, it was noticed that
the old man was missing, and one of the party immediately went to look for him.   To his surprise he found
him seated in the corner of a third class compartment.

"Hullo," he said in Gaelic, " why are you travelling third ? "

" For a hellish good reason," retorted the other.
" Just because there is no fourth."

NOT WORTHY OF HIS NAME !

This same old gentleman had several nephews,
most of whom were educated at Oxford or Cambridge.
One of those nephews was staying with him at one
time, and the old gentleman, having heard him swear
fluently in English, turned to him and said,

" Duncan, none of your forefathers lowered
themselves by swearing in English, and if you cannot
swear in good, pure Skye Gaelic, you are not worthy
of your name.   I myself speak pure Skye Gaelic, but
I don't swear in it, and neither do I so in English.   I
can inform you, however, that although Gaelic swear-

ing can often smell of brimstone and make much
mention of the devil, it never is blasphemous, filthy
or vulgar."

THE SHOCKING OF HUGH.

Hugh, an old and faithful shepherd who had
never been out of Skye, was in the employment of a
neighbour of mine—a Highlander, but one who never
used the Gaelic when speaking to his men. This
neighbour was far travelled, and had worked in the
gold mines of the Klondyke, and had also farmed in
Canada and in Australia.

One day Hugh and his master, who was rather
impatient by nature, were repairing an old wire
fence which required knotting in many parts. Hugh
held the wire while the master tied the knots, but
apparently Hugh was not doing his job satisfactorily,
and at last his master could stand it no longer and
started swearing at him in real Klondyke fashion.

" Oh, Mr. S——," said Hugh, " that is fearful.
I never heard such swearing in my life."

To this his master retorted, " Where in the Hell,
Hugh, were you ever that you heard real swearing ? "

At a later period Hugh was in my service, and I
have heard him use good strong Gaelic oaths if occasion
demanded, but "English swearing" always made his
hair stand on end.

CHAPTER II.

SAILING SMACKS—SHEEP SMEARING—
FOXES, CAIRN TERRIERS, AND OTTERS.

SAILING SMACKS.

PART of the equipment of a farm on the coast of Skye in the early nineteenth century was often a sailing smack, and now and again a four-masted sailing ship. Before the days of steamers those ships ensured that the farmer was in a position to send his stock to the nearest point on the mainland road that led to Falkirk Tryst, then the chief market for Highland live-stock. The smack also carried the annual wool-clip to Glasgow, and returned from there laden with the yearly supplies of meal and groceries, as well as with tar, grease, and oil which, on being mixed in certain proportions, made up the " ointment " with which sheep were then smeared.

SHEEP SMEARING.

This smearing took the place of dipping throughout the Highlands and Islands previous to 1880 and for some years after, and when I was a small boy I used to be deeply interested in the process of mixing the necessary amounts of Norwegian tar, grease, whale oil, and Irish butter. Those ingredients were put into tubs and very thoroughly stirred before they were considered ready for use as a " smear." The

" smearers," as the men who applied the mixture were called, were experienced men who had undergone a long and careful training. Each of them sat on a stool on which he held the sheep, in much the same manner as does a shearer, and he shed open the wool with his thumbs, and the first two fingers of both hands, beginning at the neck and working right down to the hind quarters. Then, with the first two fingers of his right hand he scooped a small quantity of the smear out of a conveniently placed tub, and spread it along the shed, pressing it hard into the sheep's skin. This went on until the whole sheep was done, including the tail and the forelock. The sheds were about two inches apart.

In a day of about twelve hours each smearer had to smear twenty sheep, and in the short winter days a good deal of his work was done by the light of *cruisgeans*, the burning oil of which was melted fat of braxy sheep. Those *cruisgeans* had as many as four wicks burning in them, and when half a dozen of them were hanging in a row from the rafters of the long smearing-house, the place seemed quite brightly lit. Many a Gaelic song and story have I listened to from the smearers as they shed their way from neck to tail.

Now and again when my father was absent from home, I was allowed to serve my apprenticeship by smearing a tail. Most of our smearers were elderly men who had smeared for many seasons in Badenoch and many other parts of the Highlands, and the stories which they had to tell about the merits of the different sheep stocks and their owners were of great interest to me.

TALES AT THE SMEARING.

One old man named " Callum Ruadh " (Red Malcolm) who had smeared with my father for many years, and who in his young days had worked in most parts of the Highlands, usually " held the floor " when reminiscences were being indulged in. I noticed that each of those men had, from amongst the masters they had served, one whom he regarded as ideal. Callum's ideal was a Badenoch tacksman who, to prove his business acumen, not only smeared his sheep heavily with cheap tar and grease to add to the weight of his annual wool-clip, but also carted two loads of fine sand to his fanks at clipping time, and ordered the wool binder to use it unsparingly.

Many a Gaelic song and story have I listened to from the smearers, and their tales of ghosts, second-sight, and *sluagh* used to strike terror into my heart. This *sluagh* was supposed to be the ghost of the funeral procession of someone who was about to die, and anyone who risked walking in the middle of the road at night time and met such a procession, was certain to be trampled under foot and badly injured. So much impressed was I by those stories told by aged smearers who fully believed them themselves, that until I was well up in my teens I always walked on the very edge of the road when I was out at night.

GAELIC SONGS.

While all those stories were being told, the smearers kept busily at their work, and sometimes, in between stories, one of them would sing a song. It is strange that though we have Gaelic songs for milking, churning, shearing, and spinning, there does not appear to be a smearing song.

Norman, one of our shepherds, often entertained the smearers with traditional songs. He possessed a beautiful natural voice, and I can still recall the charming manner in which he sang as he busily plied his smear along the shedded wool. The smearers joined heartily in the choruses. Norman was the son of a former head shepherd, and had worked in the South before succeeding his father on the latter's death.

The father was famed for owning and training collie dogs, and his strain was known far and wide. Norman had the same ability with dogs. He was also the longest-sighted man I ever came across—he could spot his sheep on a gathering day at a distance that seemed incredible, and I have seen him send his dog for some sheep that no one but he could see. He stood fully six feet in height, and was known as the fastest walker in Skye; one night, for example, he was sent to bring a doctor from Portree, just over six miles away, and he covered that distance in a few minutes under an hour.

FOREIGN TRADE.

To return to the tacksmen's schooners—some of the larger vessels also carried on a trade with foreign parts, and not very many years ago a lady—a descendant of a Skye tacksman—told me that a good deal of the furniture which I had admired in her drawing-room, had been brought from France in the four-masted sailing-ship of one of her ancestors. Not only did those gentlemen furnish their drawing-rooms from France, but they also replenished their cellars with French wines—often " duty free."

A TACKSMAN IN SKYE.

An elder brother of my father's who entered upon the lease of a tack in Skye ("tack" was the name applied to a large farm, and the tenant was therefore known as a " tacksman ") took over the sheep stock at mutual valuation, but the outgoing tenant removed all other stock, such as horses and cattle, to his new farm in the south of the island. My relation did not aspire to own a schooner, so he purchased a smack, and, in order to stock his farm with cattle and horses, he sailed across the Minch to the Outer Hebrides where my grandfather then farmed. This was late in the nineteenth century.

When my uncle arrived at his destination, my grandfather told him that he could fill his smack with any of the Highland cattle and horses that he fancied. My father then intervened and demanded that his favourite pony, " Polly," should not be allowed to go, but my grandfather's only reply was, " You can settle that between you."

THE LIFTING OF " POLLY."

After the smack had left on its return journey, my father could find no trace of " Polly," and he came to the inevitable conclusion. " Polly " was indeed on board the smack on the way to Skye. What is more, my uncle kept her, and a very useful pony she was. She would carry him the ten miles from his farm to Portree in about an hour, but she had one grave fault—it took most of the men on the farm to catch her when she was wanted, and when she was cornered she would frequently jump a five-barred gate without touching it.

After my uncle had bred some foals from her, " Polly " was again put on board the smack and along with her two-month-old filly foal was taken back to Uist. There she was delivered over to my father—an honourable return, my uncle maintained, since he was delivering two animals in place of one. The cattle reiving instincts of our clan were certainly not dormant in my uncle !

In due course my uncle died and my father succeeded him in his Skye tack. Amongst the animals he took with him from Uist was a daughter of " Polly's," and from her, sired by " Macneil's Canna," was descended my grey mare, with which I have dealt in chapter IV.

THE KINTAIL MAN'S HORSE.

The story of the " lifting " of "Polly" always reminds me of the Kintail man who came to Skye early one spring to buy a horse. After he had travelled through the island for many days without finding what he wanted, he gave up his errand as hopeless, for the Skye men would not sell their horses at a time when they were urgently needed for spring work. However, one morning before anyone but himself was astir, he spied a beautiful colt with long flowing mane and tail, tethered near the road in a township near Broadford.

The Kintail man carefully examined the horse, and decided that if the *Diabhel Sgitheanach* (Devils of Skyemen) would not take honest money for their ponies, he was now going to get one by other means. So, snatching his *sgian dubh* out of his hose, he cut the tail of the colt as near the bone as he could, roughly trimmed off the long mane, and set off leading the animal to Kylerhea ferry.

On the ferry boat one of the passengers asked the Kintail man where he had bought the pony. He answered that it was at the north end of the island, and that, owing to the season of the year, he had had to pay a ransom price for him. The passenger looked at the colt again and said,

" If your horse had a long mane and a long tail on him, I could swear that he is my colt which I left tethered at home near Broadford."

The Kintail man laughed and passed the matter off as a joke. But he was not feeling like that, and he heaved a great sigh of relief when he and the colt were safely off the ferry on the mainland. The inquisitive passenger did not feel very jocular either when he got home and found that all that remained of his colt was part of his mane and tail.

I GO TO GLENBRITTLE.

When my grey mare (see p. 167) was in her prime, I became the tenant of the extensive farm of Glenbrittle in Skye—one of the most rugged and mountainous holdings in all Scotland. I soon discovered that in the grey mare I possessed a most valuable animal for my daily work of riding over long stretches of mossy, treacherous ground and rugged hills.

I can still recall the glorious feeling of starting off on the grey mare at dawn on a June morning for a lamb marking on one of the hirsels over the hill at Loch Eynort (Bracadale). The air was loud with the morning songs of the birds, and as we climbed higher up the steep hillside, the monotonous notes of the ring-ouzel sounded above us in a deep corrie.

WATCHING A FOX.

I always associate the notes of the ring-ouzel with the many nights I spent in the corries high up in the Coolins, watching at a fox's den and ready to shoot the tenant at sight for the crime of robbing me of perhaps as many as a score of lambs—in other words, of picking my pocket of twenty golden sovereigns.

There are several varieties of the British red fox, but in Skye there is only one—the black-footed fox. This animal is similar to the other varieties on the mainland, but slightly larger, but its feet and legs are black to above the knees and hocks.

The watching of a fox den in the Coolins, often at a height of 3000 feet, is one of the coldest jobs I have ever had to do. In close proximity to a snow-wreath of last winter's snow, I have watched for several nights in succession with my faithful and game cairn terrier close beside me, and my gun at full cock ready to fire at sight. A constant companion on those vigils was the ring-ouzel, many of which breed in the Coolins. The loud, metallic, and monotonous notes of its song echoed through the corrie for the whole of the short summer night, and only stopped a little before daybreak.

An hour before daybreak, the watching party would spread out, each man taking the best cover available, so as to guard the approach to the den at all the most likely points of entry. Then we would eagerly await the return of the fox carrying home the family breakfast.

If the fox had no suspicion of danger, it approached quite openly, but on the slightest hint of anything unusual, it would come on with the greatest caution, taking all the cover it could and surveying every inch of ground from behind tufts of heather. I have watched a fox approach his den in this manner and then, when almost within gunshot, turn tail and retire to a considerable distance. When this happens, the fox hunter can rest assured that, unless the cubs in the den are very young, he has lost the best opportunity he will ever have of getting a chance shot, for never again will the fox risk coming so close. If, however, the cubs are very young, the milk begins to hurt the vixen in a day or two, and she will venture close and make desperate efforts to enter the den. Usually she then becomes an easy shot.

If the cubs are well-grown, there is still another way of attracting the vixen, and sometimes the dog fox. By muffling some rabbit traps and setting them well into the mouth of the den, the cubs can easily be caught. When this has been done, strong cords are tied round the cubs' necks and they are tethered near the place where the hunter intends to take cover. Their barking soon draws the attention of the parents. If the dog fox is the first to arrive on the scene, and if he is shot, the vixen is sure to follow, but if the vixen comes first, then the hunter can give up all hope of catching the dog.

The escape of the dog fox is a serious matter, and I myself, after having caught the vixen and cubs, have known the dog to do a great deal of lamb killing. I have heard it said that this is done as an act of revenge, but I am of opinion that he simply wanders about aimlessly and kills to pass his time, for he always leaves the lambs lying and never carries them away.

The last act in exterminating a family of foxes is to let a cairn terrier into the den to make sure that none of the cubs is still alive. I have known my old cairn terrier, " Brogach," enter and before long return and lay a dead cub at my feet. I often caught cubs alive, and they always found a ready market in England where they provided a change of blood in the hunting shires.

THE CONTENTS OF A FOX'S DEN.

To some of us it would be most interesting (although to the sheep farmer and the sportsman most annoying) to see the different animals and birds on which the fox feeds its young. I remember finding a den high up in the Coolins about the beginning of July after the cubs had been removed. My attention was attracted by the smell, and when I inspected the remnants of the carcases, I counted eighteen black-faced lambs' heads, dozens of grouse, ptarmigan, golden plovers, curlews, domestic fowls, wild duck, pheasants, rabbits, hares, rats, mice, and frogs. All this was within sight, and it would be difficult to say how much more was inside the den.

FOOD FOR THE CUBS.

It is very seldom that a fox kills lambs close to his den, and it is a strange thing that he seems to prefer blackfaced lambs to Cheviots ; I have often lost blackfaced lambs by foxes, while the neighbouring hirsel of Cheviots has lost none. Further proof is afforded by the den in which I found eighteen heads of blackfaced lambs, for there were Cheviot lambs at equal distance.

An observant shepherd can tell the age of a fox's cubs by the manner in which he kills the lambs. As soon as the cubs are able to eat, the favourite food for them is the stomach of a lamb two or three days old and full of ewe's milk. He opens up the lamb, removes the stomach, and cuts off the tail close to the body. The carcase is left lying, the contents of the stomach provide food for the cubs, and the tail is used by them as a plaything.

Ere long the cubs are ready for stronger fare, and the dog fox then carries away the whole carcase of the lamb, though as the lambs get bigger, he usually cuts the body in two, taking one half to the den and burying the other, for which he sometimes returns later. A fox has been known to kill lambs and carry them to his den nine miles away.

BROCAIRS.

In the early days of the nineteenth century when sheep farming started in the Highlands, it became necessary to destroy foxes, and for this purpose the farmers in various districts employed fox hunters called *brocairs*. Those men were paid an agreed sum by every farmer and also a capitation fee for every fox they destroyed. This determined effort at destruction was so successful that, in my young days, the fox was almost extinct in Skye, and the services of the *brocairs* were dispensed with. Within ten years, however, foxes were again to be seen in different parts of the island, and the farmers themselves, with the occasional assistance of gamekeepers, had to tackle the destruction of them.

EARLY REFERENCE TO FOXES.

The first mention of the fox (*madaidh rhua*) in Skye is in Dr. Johnson's *Journey to the Hebrides*, when, in writing of Raasay, he says :—" Hares and rabbits might be more easily obtained. That they have few or none of either in Skye, they impute to the ravages of foxes, and have therefore set for some years past a price upon their heads which, as the number was diminished, had been gradually raised from three shillings and sixpence to a guinea (in 1773). The funds for these rewards is a tax of sixpence in the pound imposed by the farmers upon themselves and said to be paid with great willingness. The foxes are bigger than those of England."

Professor Walker in his *Hebrides* (1808) writes—
" Before the year 1764 the stock of sheep in the Highlands was very confined, and that chiefly by the havoc occasioned by the fox.   In the year 1764 the gentlemen in Skye for the first time entered into a resolution to diminish the number of foxes, and for this purpose offered a premium of three shillings for each fox that was destroyed ; in consequence of this offer, no less than one hundred and twelve foxes were killed in the year 1765 in the single district of Trotterness in that Island, of which number one man destroyed thirty-seven."

THE CUNNING OF THE FOX.

It was in those days that I got the opportunity of studying the habits of the fox, which is without doubt the most cunning of all our wild animals. I had many long and weary searches in attempting to trace a fox to his den, and through time I was able to tell by the smell when I was in the neighbourhood of a den. This, however, was but the first step, for foxes often change their dens, and it still remained to find if a particular den was inhabited. This information had to be obtained by closely watching the den at daybreak and from sunset till dark, at which times the foxes returned to feed their young. We used often to have long discussions as to whether a fox came to his den down wind or up wind, and many experienced fox hunters maintained that he always came up wind. My experience is that if a fox has no suspicion of danger, it will approach its den without giving any thought to the direction of the wind, but if it is suspicious it will approach up wind.

I have shot more than one fox coming down wind, but I can particularly remember shooting an old and almost toothless dog fox on the track leading to his den and coming down wind at twenty minutes to two on a June morning. Signs of dawn were barely showing in the east, and my attention was attracted by the white tip of the animal's brush as he walked slowly along the track. I fired ahead of the white, and after a short search I found the fox lying dead with four very young rabbits and two field mice in his mouth. My old cairn terrier, who always accompanied me on those expeditions, attacked him as eagerly as if he had still been alive.

THE CAIRN TERRIER.

The cairn terrier, which in those days was known as the Skye terrier, is of great value to sheep farmers in Skye and in most hill districts in the north of Scotland. Most of us are familiar with the modern breed, but it has completely changed in appearance since the days of my boyhood, when all that mattered was that a terrier should be game and ready to face a fox or the fiercest of otters. It was also important that it should be ready to enter the deepest and roughest of cairns, so as to bolt the fox from his stronghold.

OTTER HUNTING.

The most noted strain of this breed of terrier was that of the late Captain Macdonald of Waternish in

L

Skye. Captain Macdonald was a keen sportsman and a naturalist of note, and he farmed his home farm in a manner which proved his skill not only as an agriculturist, but also as a breeder of all classes of live-stock. In his younger days he had been in the army, and not long ago I read that he was in charge of the military guard which accompanied the last convict ship to be sent to Botany Bay. His favourite sport was otter hunting, and for this he kept a considerable number of his famous cairn terriers. His estate of Waternish was well situated for this form of sport, as its long coast line and many islands contained numerous cairns where otters lived and bred. So keen was Captain Macdonald on otter hunting that he purchased the Island of Rona off the coast of North Uist simply because it was frequented by otters.

I once called on Captain Macdonald at Waternish, and as I approached the house, I was greeted by a pack of barking terriers, some of which bore traces of their fights with otters and foxes. One of them had lost a good part of his nose and lip, while another was minus an ear. This strain of Waternish terriers was famous and was keenly sought after by farmers and gamekeepers.

On his otter-hunting expeditions Captain Macdonald went round the coast on his yacht, on board which he had a pack of terriers. When a cairn came in sight, the anchor was dropped and the Captain and two or three of the terriers were rowed ashore in the dinghy. Those of his terriers who knew the different cairns would often jump overboard as soon as the dinghy grounded and swam ashore, so keen were they to reach their prey. It sometimes took the terriers quite a long time to bolt the otter, especially if he was in such a position that he could not be attacked from the rear. Because of this, the pack always included a few small-sized terriers who could enter the smaller crevices in the cairn and work their way round behind the otter.

Captain Macdonald had in his possession a tame otter which followed him about like a dog. It used to enter the sea and fish for its own food, but it always returned to its master when he called. He also had several other tame animals, including a hind which was very much attached to him.

Captain Macdonald also had a pair of white-tailed or fish eagles who would accompany him and soar high into the sky, but when he whistled to them they would swoop to him and settle beside him. They would also retrieve grouse for him when he was out shooting on the moors.

RUARIE MHOR.

My interest in fox-hunting may be traced to my early association with Ruarie Mhor (Big Rory), who was a son of one of the old *brocairs* to whom I have already referred. Rory was a gamekeeper in the neighbourhood in which I spent my boyhood. He showed distinct traces of the Scandinavian blood which is still noticeable in the population of the Western Isles, for not only was he well up to six feet in height, but he had also curly, fair hair and bright blue eyes. In build he was as lithe as an eel, and well do I remember his clean-cut ankles and sinewy but shapely calves as they appeared to me as I trotted after him while he strode through the heather when visiting his vermin traps. He used to show me with great pleasure his well-stocked vermin board on which were fox brushes and the tails of weasels, stoats, wild cats, and various birds of prey, including the golden eagle (not then protected by law).

Rory had always some interesting story about his latest capture, and he frequently told me of the days when the hen-harrier and white-tailed or fish eagle, which are now extinct, were common in Skye. The damage done to lambs by this eagle was often very great, though, strangely enough, the golden eagle, of which there are still many in Skye, rarely harms this class of stock.

A TALE OF " TAILS."

Rory had a wide beat to trap, and in the spring he usually employed a boy to help him. This boy was paid so much per head or tail, and one of them thought out an ingenious plan for increasing his earnings. He went round the crofter houses on Calidh, and many of the crofters were much puzzled to discover that their cats had mysteriously lost their tails.

BAD FOR THE HEALTH.

Rory was once having lunch with the shooting tenant on the hill. His master helped him to a good bumper of whisky in a tumbler, and then asked if he would like some water in it.

" No, no, sir," Rory replied. " Water makes me seek."

THE AGED COW.

Rory got his winter supply of beef by killing a mart which he usually bought at the Portree market in November. Now, Rory, though a good naturalist, was a poor judge of stock, and one year he met a dealer at the market, who persuaded him to buy a very old, lean cow which he passed off as a good, young fat one.

Some time later the dealer met Rory and asked how the cow had killed. Rory replied that her flesh was just like indiarubber. The dealer said that this was impossible with such a fine, young animal. At that, Rory removed his bonnet and asked the dealer to put his hand on the back of his head and feel the lump that was there.

" How did you get that ? " asked the dealer.

" I got that," answered Rory, " through your old cow. I was sitting at my dinner with my back close up to the wall, and while I was picking one of her ribs, I lost my hold."

A DIPLOMATIC MOVE.

Although Rory was no match for the dealer who sold him the cow, he had a good deal of natural shrewdness, almost bordering on cunning. In proof of this I give the following story in his own words :—

" After the sportsmen left, the wife and myself were clearing up the lodge. We took back papers and magazines to be reading, and in one of them, *The Park* or *The Field*, or some such name, we saw an advertisement saying we could get 10s for an otter. I told Lachie, the boy, to set a trap or two in the burn below the house, and sure enough the second day he caught an otter. I sent the otter away. I waited a week, but no 10s, two weeks and no 10s, a whole month and no 10s. Then I thought on a plan. I wrote a letter saying I had caught a golden eagle, and asking if they would like her alive or dead. Then P.S. very small, ' Some days ago I sent you an otter. I trust she arrived in safety.' Within four days was back a letter enclosing the 10s for the otter, and asking me to send on the eagle alive. I wrote back to say I was sorry the eagle had escaped in the meantime."

TERRIERS AND HOUNDS.

Rory had also a strain of cairn terriers descended from those kept by his father and grandfather. He was very proud of them, and was quickly jealous of any praise which might be given to Captain Macdonald's Waternish strain (see p. 153). He once told me that his father always kept a brace of fox hounds for his work. They raised the fox outside and sometimes killed him, but usually they drove him into the cairns, from where he was bolted by the terriers and shot.

CHAPTER III.

SEA-WARE—BLACK HOUSES—CARAIDHS— THE PIN-LEG TAILOR.

SEA-WARE.

The leases of some of the Skye farms which extended along the sea-coast conferred on the tenants the rights to the fore-shore. The most valuable of these was the right to gather the sea-ware which was much used as a manure in the fields. The crofters in the neighbourhood of the farms eagerly sought the privilege of gathering the sea-ware, and this was usually granted in return for labour at seed-time and harvest. The result of this and other similar privileges granted to the crofters was that the farmers got most of their work done without incurring any monetary outlay.

The cutting of the sea-ware was done at low water during the spring tides, when every available man and woman turned out with sickles to cut the dark golden clusters which grew thickly along the rugged shore. As the ware was cut it was carried in creels to the point on the beach nearest each croft, and was there built into a great heap known as *Rha toghar*, which was tightly bound together with ropes made of twisted heather. When the tide returned, those heaps, which were extremely buoyant, were towed by boat still nearer the crofts.

THE BLACK HOUSES.

In those days the majority of the crofters lived under the same roof as their cattle—a custom founded on the necessary precautions that had to be taken when cattle lifting and clan raids were common. The thatched building which accommodated both humans and cattle was primitive in the extreme, but it was as a rule situated on high ground where natural drainage was good. The only entrance was at the gable end, and the visitor had to pass through a double row of shaggy Highland cattle tied in stalls before coming to the rough wooden partition that formed one wall of the living apartment.

In the centre of the floor of the living-room was a peat fire, the smoke of which had but one means of escape—through a hole in the roof. This hole, however, was quite inadequate to deal with the volume of smoke that arose, especially from a newly-kindled fire, and the whole house, including the cattle quarters, was generally full of a dense haze. As a result of this, the wooden rafters shone as if they had been rubbed with grate polish.

The turf covering the rafters and under the thatch also got thoroughly saturated with peat smoke, and a black syrupy liquid formed in it and in damp weather dropped uncomfortably on the inmates of the house. When this happened, it was time for spring cleaning, which meant that the entire roof was removed, the rafters thoroughly scraped, and new layers of turf and thatch applied. The old turf and thatch removed from the roof made a most valuable manure when used along with sea-ware and farmyard manure, and the crofter was assured of a heavy crop of potatoes as a reward for his spring cleaning.

One point of interest about those crofter homesteads is worthy of mention—the crofter's pony was invariably housed in a separate building. This goes to prove that in the days of cattle-lifting the ponies ran wild on the hills and were seldom housed. It was only at a much later period, when horses were employed to a greater extent in farm work, that it was considered worth while to stable them.

GREAT MEN FROM HUMBLE HOMES.

It is worthy of note that under the roofs of those black houses were born many soldiers, sailors, and pioneers who brought fame to their country. Typical of these men was Angus Macmillan who was born in Crackernish near Glenbrittle early in the nineteenth century. He carried out valuable and extensive explorations in Australia, and not only have various natural features been named after him, but an annual gala day is held in his memory.

> " Reared in those dwellings have brave ones been ;
> Brave ones are still there.
> Forth from their darkness on Sunday I've seen
> Coming pure linen,
> And, like the linen, the souls were clean
> Of them that wore it."
> Sheriff Nicolson.

ONE WAY OF CATCHING SALMON.

In many of the long, narrow sea lochs of the Western Highlands and especially of Skye, there are still to be seen traces of the *caraidhs* or *yaires* which, till late in the nineteenth century, were the chief means of catching fish employed by the inhabitants of the coastal regions. They were roughly built of stone on the shore below high-water mark, and were generally semi-circular in shape. When the tide was high, the salmon and other fish swam into the *yaires*, and as they had no way of escape, they were easily captured as the water receded. Probably the last of those *yaires* to be in use was one near the head of Loch Snizort in Skye; I spent my boyhood in this neighbourhood, and, till 1895, the *yaire* was in daily use during the season.

I have on many occasions watched this ancient mode of fishing, which began annually in May and continued till November or even later, according to the herring season. Salmon were fished from May till the end of August, and then there was a lull till the end of September when the herring shoals came up the lochs from the open sea. The fishing took place at each receding tide, the *caraidh* being entered as soon as the water had fallen sufficiently to ensure the imprisonment of the fish within the sea-weed covered walls. The frame of the *lub* or landing-net was made of a hazel or ash sapling, and was oblong in shape—about sixty inches in length by twenty-four inches in width. One end was rounded off to a blunt point, and about twenty inches from this was a cross bar. To this frame was attached a small bag net about eighteen inches deep. The fisherman held the blunt end in one hand and the cross-bar in the other, and stood ready to scoop out the fish as they entered the net.

The fishers, both male and female, usually arrived at the *yaire* some time before it was possible to begin operations, and waited in the shelter of a grassy bank till the appearance of a certain rock above the water showed that the tide had fallen sufficiently. The signal to start fishing was generally given by a tailor with a pin-leg, who was recognised as the most expert fisher, and when he gave the word the entire company entered the water and waded towards the *yaire*. As they advanced, the water got gradually deeper and frequently it came up to their arm-pits. Each of the fishers held his or her net deep down in the water in a slanting position, and whenever a fish struck the bag, the whole landing net was lifted above the surface and carried ashore, where the fish was knocked on the head.

It was not uncommon to catch up to 100 salmon at one tide, while in the herring season I have seen as many as forty crans taken. Such fisheries were of great advantage to the poor crofters who not only obtained their winter supply of salt herring at little or no cost, but also got some much-needed money from the sale of the salmon, though, indeed, those rarely realised more than sixpence a pound.

THE PIN-LEG TAILOR.

The tailor with the pin-leg was a man of considerable individuality and his skill as a *caraidh* fisherman was known throughout Skye. On one occasion a local landowner had laid down oyster beds on one of his foreshores, and had posted the usual warning notices. The tailor, however, refused to pay any attention to them and consistently helped himself to the oysters. The inevitable happened—he was taken to court at Portree and sentenced to several days' imprisonment.

The day after his release the tailor was seen waiting for the tide to ebb so that he might gather his daily supply of shell-fish as his forebears had done for generations. The Gaelic motto, " *Seas gu Dluth ri Cliu do Shinnsir* " (" Stand fast for the rights of your fore-fathers "), was strong in him. This time, however, he was allowed to continue in his defiance. As a matter of fact, the notice boards were soon removed and the preservation of the oyster beds ended, for the landowner discovered that he was not likely to realise his dreams of immense profits.

This tailor came of true Highland fighting stock— one of his forebears was killed at Culloden, and a grand-uncle stood in Sir Colin Campbell's " Thin Red Line " at Balaclava. He himself often maintained that only the loss of his leg in early youth had prevented him from becoming a soldier, and certainly, apart from his leg and a poor school education, he lacked none of the attributes of a great general.

Despite his physical infirmity, the tailor was an active and willing helper at hay-making and more especially at the making of the *dais*—the long hay-stack into which was put the whole of the season's crop. I used to be greatly amused by the tailor's antics when the *dais* grew to such a height that he had difficulty in delivering his forkfuls ; he would leap off the ground in his efforts to reach the top, and when he came to earth again his wooden leg would sink deeply into the soft soil.

At the annual harvest home the tailor was always a welcome guest, and after he had freely sampled the contents of the wicker-clad five-gallon greybeard, there was no one more ready to sing a song, tell a story, or join in a dance. At this last his leg was a definite menace to all the other merrymakers.

Incidentally, the five-gallon greybeard contained whisky which was bought by my father from a spirit merchant in Greenock at 17s per proof gallon. A third part of water was added to each gallon, and the whisky was still more potent than that which is sold at the present day.

THE BROKEN LEG.

There was one of his exploits that the tailor never tired of describing. In those days few markets passed without some disagreement that ended in a set fight, and on one occasion the tailor found himself taking a leading part in a brawl. He soon knocked out his adversary, however, and then retired to join his friends in the tap-room of one of the hotels. The friends of the vanquished man followed him and advanced into the room to attack him. Quickly realising his danger, the tailor jumped into the nearest corner of the room, put his back to the wall and unstrapped his wooden leg for use as a weapon of defence. Soon he was hopping about on one leg and brandishing the other in the air, and almost ere the fight had properly begun he had cleared the room of his enemies. As the last of the attackers was making his escape through the door, the tailor brought his wooden leg down with such force on his buttocks that it broke in two. Many years afterwards I heard him telling the story, and as proof he showed the neatly-mended break in the leg.

CHAPTER IV.

MY FAITHFUL GREY MARE.

ONE of the finest Highland ponies I ever possessed was a grey mare descended from a strain of ponies that my family had owned for many generations. When young she was of a dappled grey colour, but as she advanced in years she became snow-white. She was about 14·2 hands in height, had a small Arab-looking head, fine long neck, and slanting riding shoulders, and her eyes showed that bold, yet docile, and intelligent look which characterises her breed.

The first of the strain was owned by my grandfather in the Outer Isles, and my father always maintained that she was descended from " Boisdale's Ponies "—the name usually applied to the descendants of the Spanish horses brought to Uist by Clanranald about 1712. This I have dealt with in full in Part I., Chapter II.

HOLIDAYS ON HORSEBACK.

Some of the most enjoyable holidays I have ever had were spent on the back of my grey mare, and I am fully convinced that, even to-day, there is no better way of seeing the secluded beauty spots of the Highlands and Islands of Scotland than in a saddle on a sure-footed Highland pony. The roughest and the softest of tracks through the glens, the steepest of hills,

and the most turbulent rivers and burns are but
trifling obstacles to those docile and intelligent animals.
Many of the happiest days of my life have been spent
in this manner, and I earnestly commend it to all who
want to know the meaning of real pleasure when on
holiday.

ON HORSEBACK THROUGH UIST.

One beautiful morning early in the present
century, I left my home at Duntulm in Skye, where I
farmed for eleven years before it was turned into a
small-holding settlement, and rode my grey mare over
the nine miles to Uig.   There we boarded the
steamer *Locheil* which carried us across the Minch
to Lochmaddy in North Uist.

I was soon riding along the winding, but not
hilly, road through North Uist, pausing now and again
to watch the trout rising in one or other of the in-
numerable lochs which, owing to the peaty nature of
the soil, are noticeably brown in colour.

I was particularly interested in the sheep, which
in their sharp pointed faces showed distinct traces of
the small native sheep known as the *caora beag*.   As a
matter of fact, there still survive in Uist the remnants
of the *caora beag* which stocked our hills previous
to the latter half of the eighteenth century, when they
were displaced by the Cheviot and the Linton or
Tweeddale breeds, the names used for the modern
black-faced breed by James Macdonald in his
General View of the Agriculture of the Hebrides,
published in 1811.   It seems that the first improved
breed of sheep introduced to the Hebrides came

from West Linton in Peebles-shire where one of the largest sheep fairs in the South of Scotland was held annually in the month of June. Imported stock also came from the neighbouring district of Tweeddale. About the middle of the nineteenth century, West Linton sheep market was the main source of supply for stocking the Highland hills, for the Highlanders at that period were inexperienced with sheep and kept no breeding stock. Each spring, therefore, they came to West Linton Fair and bought wedder hoggs, which, after being kept for two or three years, were sold at Perth. Through time the Highland demand for breeding stock increased, with the result that West Linton started a fair for ewe hoggs in April, and most of the animals exposed there found their way to the Highlands. In course of time the Highlanders began to breed their own stock, and their visits to West Linton fairs ceased.

THE NORTH FORD.

My way through North Uist soon brought me to the North Ford where at low water three miles of firm white sand join Uist and Benbecula. A native to whom I spoke informed me that the ford was now crossable, and would remain so for the next two hours. I had not gone far on my way when I noticed by the tracks on the sand that I was preceded by a horse and cart, but in the summer haze which hung over the locality, I failed to catch sight of them.

As the sand was dry and firm, a more tempting place for a gallop could not be imagined, and soon the grey mare was galloping silently along. Before

M

long we made up on the horse and cart, and followed behind them for the rest of our journey across the sands.

SEA-BIRDS.

I was much interested by the various types of sea-birds to be seen at the Ford.   The Arctic tern flew querulously above our heads, while there were also oyster-catchers, sandpipers, and numerous species of gulls, some resting on the sands with their necks deeply sunk into their breasts, others flying anxiously looking for food.   On a black projecting stone stood a large black-backed gull, occasionally uttering that familiar " clack " which strikes terror into the young of all feathered creatures.   This bird is supposed to be the most cruel of all our British birds—and this opinion is justified, for I have several times seen one of them attack a fallen ewe and, after picking out her eyes and tongue, turn on her lamb and treat it in similar fashion.   They have also been known to swoop down amongst a brood of chickens and carry one away, swallowing it alive whilst still on the wing.   There are numerous islands off the Outer Hebrides on which they breed in colonies, sometimes numbering up to a score.   As I rode past this handsome bird, I could not fail to notice the cold, callous look in its eye.

DANGER AT THE SOUTH FORD.

I was lucky in my crossing of the North Ford, for it was dead low water and the spring tides were at their height.   It was not long before my mare and I left the sands and took to the road that runs through Benbecula. We had an uneventful journey, and at nightfall we reached Creagorry Hotel on the bank of the South Ford between Benbecula and South Uist. We stayed there for the night, and next morning I was told by the hotel proprietor that the ford would be passable about eleven o'clock—this information I afterwards found to be incorrect, and it might have cost me my life.

Shortly after eleven, then, I set off along the rough cart track leading to the sands, and I was soon galloping to the edge of the ford. My mare was walking quietly along with the water up to her knees, when she suddenly dived head first, carrying me with her, into deep water that came up to my armpits. However, when her hooves struck the sandy bottom, her head again appeared on the surface, and she started to swim strongly.

To relieve her of my weight, I got out of the saddle and held on to the pommel with my right hand, while with my left I swam beside her. At last we touched the bottom on the opposite side, and after climbing a few steps up a steep bank, we landed safely on the firm white sands. You may be sure that before I remounted and made for the road through South Uist, I gave my mare a fervent word of encouragement and a friendly clap on her grey neck.

I learned afterwards that I had attempted to cross the ford too soon—if I had waited for another half hour till the tide had receded, I would have crossed in complete safety.

SOUTH UIST.

It is said that in the island of South Uist the area of fresh water exceeds that of solid land. The main road runs through the centre of Loch Bee, the water of which passes through culverts under the road. This is the largest loch in the island, and studded through it are many attractive islets which form sanctuaries for numerous species of water fowl. One cannot fail to notice the number of swans on this loch—it is not an uncommon sight to see as many as fifty in one lot, and as we were passing on this particular day, about twenty of them rose on the wing and, after circling round our heads, flew gracefully southwards. On one of the islets near the road I saw a swan sitting closely on her eggs, the nest consisting of dry heather and reeds. A native told me that he knew of a boy who had had his arm broken by a blow from a swan's wing when he was trying to remove her eggs from under her.

After Loch Bee, the road passes a loch containing an islet on which grows the only tree in the whole of Uist. It is many years since I first saw this " Monkey's Puzzle," but I have seen no change in its growth. There may well be truth in the story of the youth from Uist, on landing from the steamer at Dunvegan one dark night and going through a thick-hanging beech avenue, asked his companion if they were in a cave in the earth !

My way soon took me to the home of a relation who then farmed a large part of the land now under small-holdings. I stayed with him for several days, and had many interesting rides on the beautiful machair land and on the white strands that skirt it.

KELP.

In the late spring huge quantities of sea tangle are driven ashore on these strands. This tangle was, at the time of which I am writing, a valuable asset to the crofter. He carted it with his Highland pony on to the machair, and stacked it on stone dykes to dry. He then burned it and put the ashes, or kelp, into bags which he despatched to the South, where iodine and other valuable chemicals were extracted. Kelp was also used in the manufacture of glass. The revenue derived from this industry was at this time very large, but now kelp burning is a thing of the past. James Macdonald in his *Survey of the Agriculture of the Hebrides* (published in 1811) mentions that the revenue derived from kelp amounted to £60,000 per annum, and in some seasons to as much as £80,000.

FLORA MACDONALD'S BIRTHPLACE.

On one of my expeditions from my relation's farm, I visited the ruins of the house where Flora Macdonald, the heroine of the 'Forty-five, was born, and I also went to see Ormaclett Castle, which belonged to her cousin, the Chief of Clanranald, and where she received her early education from one of the family tutors.

After spending a few days in making these and other expeditions, I continued on my way to Lochboisdale where I joined the steamer for Dunvegan and home.

A RIDE THROUGH SUTHERLAND.

The following summer I took the steamer from Portree to Lochinver in Wester Sutherland, and from there I rode as far north as Drumbeg on Eddrachillis Bay, returning the same day to Culag Hotel, a few miles south of Lochinver. This fine building was once the residence of one of the Dukes of Sutherland, but it is now a luxurious hotel mainly for anglers, many of whom come there as regularly as do the migrating birds. Some of the men who congregated in the smoking-room after dinner were friendly, but one or two made me feel as if I was an intruder. The talk touched on many subjects, but it always drifted back to fishing, and I found great satisfaction in the thought that I was possessed of a skill in procuring salmon that no one else in the room had. This I had acquired from Hector the Blacksmith.

HECTOR THE BLACKSMITH.

My long friendship with Hector dates back to the days when, clad in my clan tartan kilt, I used to hold my school pony while it was shod, and while Hector cursed in Gaelic the hard-wearing qualities of her shapely hooves. Hector was not only a good tradesman, but he was also a keen shot, and he had my father's permission to shoot rabbits whenever he felt inclined. It was more than rabbit fur, however, that I one day noticed adhering to Hector's game bag!

On his shooting expeditions he was always accompanied by his faithful Cairn terrier, Murrachah, which he had trained to set on all game as steadily as the best of Gordon setters, to retrieve on sea and land, and to attack savagely and bolt a fox or otter out of the deepest and roughest cairn.

Through having gained Hector's confidence, I often had the privilege of accompanying him, and I remember one occasion when I returned after long hours of varied sport, with my knees deeply scratched and my kilt badly torn by the briars and brambles through which I had followed Hector and Murrachah. My mother sternly reprimanded me, decreeing that this would have to end and that I was on no account to go with Hector again.

SPEARING SALMON.

There was one form of sport in which Hector really excelled, and that was salmon spearing. By reason of his trade he was a master hand at making spears, and although he had made many of various types—with one, two or three prongs—he found those with one prong the best, especially in deep water where the best fish are always to be found. Spear heads for this purpose are made of steel and are about six or eight inches long. From this steel protrudes one and sometimes two spurs to prevent the fish from slipping off after it is struck. The head is fixed on to a light, strong pole from twelve to fifteen feet long.

The keenness of Hector's eye-sight was almost incredible ; he could spot a salmon at a fair depth in water that was not too clear, when I, even with

his guidance, had great difficulty in seeing it.   His aim
was deadly, and he rarely missed a fish.

I have vivid memories of an August day when
between us we grassed six salmon of various sizes.
The day was dull to start with, the light was far from
good, and we had to travel a long way before we came
upon our first fish.   At last Hector spotted a salmon
and signalled to me to come and have a look at it.
Although I had great trouble in seeing it, Hector
soon had it flapping on the grass on the bank.

We saw another fish in the next pool, and as it
was lying in a good position, Hector insisted that I
should have a shot at it.   Holding the spear as he
had taught me, I took careful aim and struck.   To my
horror I saw the pole go floating down the river—in
my excitement I had lost my hold.

After Hector had landed three more fish, he again
asked me to try my luck.   This time I struck my fish
some distance behind the gills, and Hector seemed
more pleased than I was.   After that I got along
fairly well, but I was never able to spot fish with
anything like Hector's ability.

Salmon spearing and falconry are amongst the
oldest of sports, though I am afraid that salmon spearing would not be called that nowadays.   Much
mention is made of it by the ancient Gaelic bards.
Long experience, keen eyesight, and a true aim are
the necessary qualities for success, and even when the
" spearsman " possesses all these the salmon still
has a reasonable chance of beating him.

THE WAY TO ULLAPOOL.

On the morning after the gathering in the smoking room of the Culag Hotel, my grey mare was brought round by one of the grooms. I happened on this occasion to have her hogg-maned, and when I came out of the hotel, one of my friends of the previous evening stood clapping her neck.

" I notice," he said, " That all this breed of ponies with short manes are good."

I heartily agreed, though his opinion was of about as much value as anything I might have to say about the innermost workings of a motor-car engine !

I continued my journey by the coast road to Ullapool, and a rougher and more undulating road I never experienced. I passed several crofter townships, and though the houses looked comfortable and the patches of arable land seemed well cultivated, the hill pastures were poor and had little or no grass.

In recent years the native Highland cattle in Wester Ross-shire have been replaced by the polled black Angus breed, and the lean black hornless animals looked to me to be ill-suited to their surroundings. I am of opinion that the native breed of cattle should be preserved in those parts, for they are a decided asset and no other breed can adequately replace them or their crosses.

ACROSS LOCH BROOM.

Late in the evening I arrived at Ullapool, a sleepy village on the shore of beautiful Loch Broom. After seeing my mare comfortably stabled, I asked the distance to Gairloch round the head of the loch, and found that I would be hard-pressed for time if I was to catch the steamer there for Portree the next afternoon. It then occurred to me that by swimming my mare across Loch Broom I would save nearly thirty miles. A fisherman who was mending his nets on the beach told me that he had lived all his life in the district, and had never heard of anyone swimming a horse across the loch. He added that no one in his senses would even think of doing such a thing.

I discussed my project with him, however, but he gave me little encouragement. All the same, before we parted for the night he agreed to ferry me over next morning, but was very careful to state that he accepted no responsibility for my mare.

The next day was gloriously fine, and as I rode my grey mare to the beach, life seemed very sweet. My cautious fisherman was ready with his boat, and after I had unsaddled the mare, he gave me a rope with which to make a halter. Taking the loose end of the halter, I stepped into the stern of the boat, and when the fisherman began to row, the grey mare walked confidently into the water. Soon she was swimming strongly close up to the stern, and in next to no time we were at the other side and she was walking lightly up the shingle, looking as if she knew that she had lived up to my clan motto—*Air Muir 's air Tir* (By Sea and Land). After her refreshing morning swim, she soon covered the miles to Gairloch, where we boarded the *Claymore* for Portree.

FAREWELL TO THE GREY MARE.

I have tried to describe a few of the happy days I spent mounted on my grey mare, and now I must finish my story of our long companionship. Early one June morning I found her stretched out on the dewy grass—her stout, brave heart had ceased to beat, and cruel old age had taken its toll. I stood over her with bent head, and my tears damped her snow-white coat. Reverently we buried her that evening, digging her grave deep in the sandy loam of the wide meadow over which she had so often galloped. The jagged peaks of the blue Coolins stood over us like sentinels, and the crimson sun sinking solemnly into the blue seas beyond the Hebrides seemed to fit into my mood. A more faithful, sagacious, and lovable animal never trod on four shoes.

CHAPTER V.

THE HOMING INSTINCT IN ANIMALS AND NOTES ON THE ROARING OF STAGS AND ON THE DISTANCE THAT A STAG CAN SWIM.

HOMING INSTINCTS.

THE homing instincts of many of our domestic animals have often been commented upon. They are well-developed in the Highland pony, though not perhaps so highly as in the mountain breed of sheep and in the collie dog.

UIST PONIES LONG FOR HOME.

A Skye horse-dealer who used to buy ponies at the Uist markets and take them by steamer to Portree told me that often some of them on straying found their way to Waternish Point, the nearest point in Skye to Uist. When he had any difficulty in tracing strays, he made straight for this Point, where he could depend on finding them close to the edge of the sea and looking longingly across the stormy Minch to their native island. The strange thing is that Waternish Point was at least fifty miles from the dealer's home, and in between lay many obstacles such as sea lochs, fences, and crofters' townships. The dealer maintained that some of the ponies took short cuts to the Point and even swam one of the sea lochs where it was narrowest.

THE HOMING COLLIE.

The pride of place amongst homing animals must, however, be given to a collie dog which was owned by a shepherd in the service of a prominent Skye farmer. This shepherd, with the assistance of his collie, drove his master's annual draft of sheep to be sold at the September Tryst at Falkirk. At one Tryst, a Cumberland farmer was attracted by the wonderful wisdom of the dog and his capacity for work, and managed to persuade the shepherd to sell him.

When the shepherd arrived home, his master was most displeased that he had sold the dog, and remarked that if he had hired himself to the " Sassenach " and sent the dog back home with one of the assistant shepherds, there would have been no harm done !

A few weeks passed, and one morning the shepherd opened the door of his cottage to find his faithful collie on the step. The dog had probably found his way back to Falkirk from the South, and then taken the familiar westward road, and he must have swum across Kylerhea, which separates Skye from the mainland.

At the next Tryst, the dog drew the attention of a Lanarkshire farmer, and the shepherd succumbed to his offer of a big price. The anger of his master when he returned home knew no bounds, and he decided to dismiss the shepherd on the spot. The shepherd reasoned with him, however, and as he assured his master that the dog would soon be home, the matter was allowed to drop. In less than a week the collie was again awaiting the opening of the cottage door.

This ended the dog's visits to the Trysts, for the master, probably out of admiration for the dog, insisted that he should never again accompany the shepherd to the mainland.

THE ROARING OF STAGS.

One of the leading authorities on wild life in Scotland, and more especially on the red deer, stated recently in a wireless talk that he had himself heard the roaring of stags during the rutting season at a distance of twenty-two miles across the sea, and that he knew of a case where they had been heard thirty miles away. My experience does not bear this out, for when I rented the island of Muck, about ten miles south of Rhum, neither I (and I lived there frequently, though not permanently) nor anyone else on the island ever heard the roaring of stags from Rhum.

A STAG'S SWIM.

I can record definite proof of the distance that stags can swim; while I was tenant of Muck, I had in my employment a shepherd, called Charles Macdonald, who told me that some years before I took over the tenancy, he had come across a stag lying in a natural position some yards above high water-mark. The animal was dead but his mouth contained some partly chewed grass. The part of the island where he lay was directly opposite Rhum, and Macdonald maintained that he had swum from there, walked a few yards on to the grass, and then died of exhaustion.

CHAPTER VI.

STORIES OF "BLUE SANDY" AND SOME NOTES ON HIGHLAND FUNERALS.

"BLUE SANDY."

IN the old days in Skye rents were collected on the market day in one of the rooms of the village hotel. It was the custom for the estate factor to entertain the important farmers to a sumptuous luncheon, while each of the crofters received a glass of whisky and a biscuit when he paid his rent.

When I was a boy, there lived in Skye a well-known character called "Blue Sandy." He usually invited himself to all social functions, and he never failed to arrive at the factor's rent-day luncheon. Unlike most tramps, he had a very proud nature and disliked gossip so much that he would quickly show displeasure if asked about the goings-on at the farm at which he had spent the previous night. His desire to be secretive about his movements was also noticeable, and his displeasure was easily aroused when anyone asked where he was coming from or where he was going to.

A RENT-DAY LUNCHEON.

On one occasion the luncheon took place as usual in the village hotel, and was presided over by

the factor—a descendant of the family of Corry-
Chattanach, where Dr. Johnson spent a night and
rebuked Boswell next morning for sitting too long
over the punch bowl with his host and young Maclean
of Coll. The meal was over, glasses had been filled,
and toasts were being drunk, when the door opened
and in walked " Blue Sandy." He calmly took a
chair and sat well into the large peat fire which was
blazing in the grate behind the chairman. The toast
which was in progress when he entered having been
honoured, Sandy was, on Corry's instructions, provided with a large glass of whisky. After a few more
toasts had been proposed and replied to, Corry
turned to Sandy, who was now perspiring freely, and
said in his soft, gentlemanly voice,

" May I ask, Sandy, where you have come from
to-day ? "

" By your leave, Corry," Sandy replied, " I
have just come straight from Hell."

This answer caused a great deal of amusement
among the guests, and Corry decided that it might
be profitable to continue the conversation. So he
asked,

" And may I ask, Sandy, how things are in Hell ?"

" Oh, Corry," was the quick reply, " Just the
same as they are here—the rich men sweltering inside,
and the poor men shivering outside."

SANDY AND THE GIGOT.

Sandy once called at Corry's house, and, when
he was leaving, the cook presented him with what
remained of a gigot of mutton. Sandy at once began

to eat it, and before he had gone far on his road the gigot had arrived at the stage when he held the bare bone and picked off the scraps of meat with his teeth. Suddenly at a sharp bend of the road he came face to face with the local clergyman to whom he had a strong dislike. The clergyman rebuked him for going along the public road picking a bone in this way and strongly commanded him to throw the bone to the first dog he met.

" There it is to you, then," said Sandy, throwing the gigot at the clergyman's feet.

A HARVEST HOME.

In the olden days the clan chiefs kept a retinue which always included a " jester," and if Sandy had only lived then, he would without doubt have filled that responsible post with the Chief of the Macdonalds. Even in his own day Sandy was a welcome guest at every mansion and cottage in Skye.

At that time there lived in retirement in Skye several Anglo-Indians who, after having amassed considerable fortunes in the East, had returned to end their lives in their native island. Sandy found it to his advantage to pay frequent visits to those gentlemen of wealth and leisure, and once, after one such call, he came on to our annual " harvest home." On his head he wore a white sun-helmet, and his well-cut lounge suit had obviously come from the shop of one of London's most exclusive tailors. When we boys saw him coming along the road to our home straining against a November gale, we prepared for mischief.

N

The feast, which was one of the main items of the celebrations, was served in the large barn, and Sandy seated himself, not at the large table, but at a smaller side table. He was joined there by several of the younger guests who were bent on having some fun with his helmet. He, however, was cautious, and placed the helmet between his knees where he held it firmly. As he was the oldest man at the table it fell to him to say grace before meat, and he broke forth with gusto into what was a prayer rather than a grace. After praying for a blessing to be bestowed upon his host and hostess, he finished up by asking that the food and drink might also be blessed, and in an earnest voice concluded, " and more especially the drink. Amen."

ONE UP ON THE MINISTER.

On another occasion Sandy visited the minister to whom he had presented the gigot bone, and when he announced that he would spend the night at the manse, his host showed him to his bed in the stable loft. When they arrived at the foot of the ladder leading to the loft, the clergyman remarked that Sandy would now find his own way to his bed which he was sure would be most comfortable. Sandy, however, insisted that his host should climb the ladder and satisfy himself that the bed was all he represented it to be.

So the clergyman started to climb, and as soon as he took his foot off the last step, Sandy withdrew the ladder and, bidding him good-night, expressed the hope that he would enjoy the comfort of the bed of which he spoke so highly. Sandy himself found his way back to the manse and passed the night in the minister's own bed.

HIGHLAND FUNERALS.

Sandy attended all the funerals and weddings that he could, and once he was heard to remark on his return from a funeral, " Give me a funeral during the day and a wedding during the night." Needless to say he meant both those ceremonies to be " Highland " !

A Highland funeral in byegone days was a ceremony of considerable importance, partly because of the long distance over which the coffins had to be carried to the burying places. Highlanders, although much attached to their ponies, would on no account use them for funeral purposes as it was considered a slight on the dead to carry his corpse by any other means than by relays of friends and neighbours. This meant that the entire male population of a district was invited to a funeral, and that most of them attended.

The custom was that the nearest relations and members of the dead man's clan took the first relay on leaving his home and the last relay on entering the grave-yard, while the remainder of the mourners took the intervening relays. At the rear of the procession came a Highland pony yoked to a cart containing food and refreshments to sustain the company during what was often a long and trying journey. Frequent halts were made to partake of those refreshments, and at each halting-place a cairn of stones was roughly built as a memorial to the dead man. To this day there are many of those cairns along the public highways of the Outer Islands. There must, for example, be scores of them along the road between Tarbert Harris and the burying ground in Scarasta.

When the cortege arrived at the grave-yard, the grave had still to be dug, and this could not be done until the *reilig* (lair) had been decided upon by the friends of the deceased who had an intimate knowledge of the genealogy of his family. A decision having been arrived at, many willing members of the party soon completed the digging of the grave.

PRAISE OF THE DEAD.

After the burial was over, each and all settled down in the grave-yard to partake of some sustenance. A rite known in Gaelic as *moladh mairbh* (praise of the dead) was then celebrated, and as refreshments came round frequently, the well-known eloquence of the Celtic race was more exuberant than ever. This rite was handed down from the days when the clan system was in vogue and many Highlanders performed deeds of valour before they died. Clan fights and cattle reiving provided material for *moladh mairbh*, which was lacking in a later and more prosaic age.

The last time I heard of this rite being observed was at the burial of a man who had had many vices and few if any good qualities. A call was made for *moladh mairbh* but no one responded, until at last one man got up and eloquently descanted on his departed friend's capacity as a smoker of tobacco.

AFTER THE FUNERAL.

Once when I was a small boy, three members of a funeral party arrived at our house after the ceremony. As they had travelled a long way, they were prevailed on to spend the night with us. One of the party was a layman who was a fluent preacher, and my father, who always held family worship, asked him, out of respect for his gift of oratory, to take the service. By the time a " chapter " had been read and a Psalm sung, the other two members of the funeral party had begun to show signs of exhaustion.

Then the company got down on their knees, and the layman began an interminable prayer. His eloquence seemed to carry him away and the words flowed from him like the waters of a flooded mountain torrent. At long last the end came and we rose to our feet, but to my horror the two funeral guests remained on their knees fast asleep. The combination of long journey, hot sun, unstinted refreshments, and oratorical gymnastics had been too much for them.

BAGPIPES AT FUNERALS.

Before the Disruption in 1843 Highland funerals were usually preceded by a piper, but after that date most of the Free Church clergy condemned all forms of amusement, and especially the playing of the bagpipes. Indeed, the pipes were roundly denounced from the pulpits as " an instrument of the devil." I have been told that in at least one parish in Skye, the minister ordered all the bagpipes to be collected, and then had a bonfire made of them.

The use of bagpipes at funerals certainly did lead to occasional unseemly incidents, particularly when refreshments were served in the usual liberal fashion. At one funeral the piper who headed the procession had indulged too freely, and instead of playing the sad but appropriate and very beautiful laments, he struck up *Calum Crubach*, one of the most lightsome and cheerful of dancing tunes. Perhaps, therefore, the Free Church ban was fully justifiable !

HIGHLAND WEDDINGS.

The bagpipes were also used at weddings, particularly in the islands of Barra and South Úist where they were not frowned upon as they were in Skye and other Protestant islands. When I was a small boy I once saw a wedding party in Barra marching to the chapel preceded by a piper, the bride and her bridesmaid coming immediately after him, then the groom and groomsman, and then the rest of the party, two deep. The bride was dressed in the latest fashion of the time—a dress of brightly striped homespun drugget and a heavily fringed shawl of her own clan tartan which hung three corner ways over her shoulder, one of the corners almost touching her heels. Round her head was wound a small shawl of the clan tartan of her future husband. When the procession reached the chapel, the piper stood at the door and played everyone in.

After the ceremony, the procession left the chapel in the same order and marched back to the home of the bride, where the wedding feast was held. The principal course consisted of the fowls which had been presented to the bride as wedding gifts. Those fowls, like most gift birds, were usually old and tough, and I well remember how this was illustrated at a wedding feast which I attended. We were sitting at a long table and opposite me was a man to whom was given the honour of carving an ancient bird. He struggled with it manfully, but it resisted all his efforts and, slipping off the plate, shot across the table, struck the man next me fair on the chest, and slipped between his knees on to the floor. He lifted it, and as he handed it back across the table the carver remarked in Gaelic, " The man who killed such a young and tender chicken was nothing but a cruel monster."

After the feast was over, the party usually retired to a barn where dancing took place. The young men always made a point of having a good supply of the sweets called " Conversation Lozenges," on which were printed a variety of sentiments, mainly of an amatory nature. Many a youth found those sweets an invaluable means of revealing his secret love for some fair maid.

Dancing and singing went on till late in the following morning.

A HIGHLAND BAPTISM.

Mention of funerals and weddings calls to my mind an incident connected with baptism and I think that it may be of interest. Black Neil (*Neall Dubh*) was a shepherd on one of the wildest and most remote hirsels of the Coolin Hills. His home, which was little better than a primitive sheiling, was situated in a deep, gloomy corrie far distant from any other habitation, and seldom did his wife and family see a stranger. I once met Neil when he was on his rounds accompanied by two collies and four small children, and as soon as they saw me the children disappeared into the bracken like a covey of young grouse. I remarked on their shyness and Neil said that they took it from him, for he was exactly the same at their age. At that time he had five of a family, the eldest being eight years old, and none of them had ever been at school or out of sight of their isolated home.

Shortly afterwards, Neil thought that the children should be baptised, so he arranged that the minister should come and perform the ceremony. When the children saw him approaching, however, they bolted under the box bed and nothing would induce them to come out. Neil and his wife were both stoutly built and they found it quite impossible to squeeze in after the children. Then Neil had a bright idea— he took his long crooked *cromag* (walking-stick) and by hooking it round their necks as he did with young lambs, he pulled the children out one by one and held them fast while the minister named them. When the children were released they bolted out of the house, and did not appear again till the minister was far down the glen on his homeward way.

CHAPTER VII.

MAIL COACHES IN SKYE.

I CAN recall the days when the mail coaches in Skye were horsed by stout Skye-bred ponies, mostly of Highland blood. I travelled by those coaches on many occasions, and for real discomfort they would have been hard to beat. It would be difficult for me to give in cold print any adequate description of the hardships under which people travelled in those far-distant days, but I will try to give an account of a typical journey by coach.

A TYPICAL JOURNEY BY COACH.

Some routes were more famed than others for discomfort, but the most notable of all was that from Portree to Dunvegan. I remember one evening when eight passengers, all of them men, climbed on to the top of this coach and took their seats. I followed, and, being the youngest of the company, had to sit on the top of a mail basket, where I was exposed to all the elements. The night was dark, and the wind blew strong from the north-west with heavy showers of cold rain. We had not travelled far when one of those drenching showers soon penetrated any protection I had, and there I sat with the cheerful prospect of getting still wetter as each succeeding shower blew up. The thought of sitting perched on this hamper for the next three hours was anything but cheerful, but the monotony, and to a certain extent the discomfort, were relieved when we arrived at the bottom of the first steep hill, where we were ordered by the driver to dismount and continue our journey on foot. On arriving at the top of the hill we again got on to the coach, and our pair of sturdy horses trotted steadily along till we came to a roadside post office where we had to deliver and collect letters.

SONGS AND GOOD CHEER.

It was common at that period for the Postmaster not only to look after Her Majesty's mails, but also to keep the local inn. So, what was more natural than that my travelling companions and the driver should retire into the inn for some refreshments, while I remained seated on my hamper and shivering with cold.

Soon we resumed our journey, and in spite of one of the heaviest showers yet experienced, my travelling companions were now quite cheerful. They talked and joked, and at last one of them was persuaded to sing a Gaelic song. This song of many verses was sung to a most plaintive air quite out of keeping with the mood of the audience, but they all joined lustily in the chorus. The trials of an unfaithful lover and a broken-hearted swain were still being narrated when we had to get down at the foot of a long hill. This having been climbed, we had hardly remounted when another Post Office and inn combined hove in sight and the company entered in search of " something to warm us."

We were soon on our way again, and this time it seemed as if nothing would ever damp the good cheer of my companions—not even the torrential showers which were more frequent than ever. It was decided that one stalwart traveller must sing a song, and after a good deal of coaxing he broke forth in a voice which, if not musical, was so powerful that it drowned the rattle of our crude conveyance, and echoed through the mists that covered the hills on either side of the road. The song, most appropriately, was in praise of whisky. It described its virtue as a cure for almost all ailments, and stated that, no matter how deep a man's mental depression might be, whisky would soon brighten his outlook. Judging by the enthusiastic reception of the song, it was evident that the audience was in complete agreement with its sentiments.

We came to our journey's end at last, and I seldom sit in a modern omnibus but I think of that night and of the discomforts that had to be endured on the mail coaches of thirty years ago.

CHAPTER VIII.

A GENTLEMAN OF THE OLD SCHOOL.

One of the most prominent breeders of Highland cattle of his day was Mr. Stewart, Laird of the island of Ensay and tenant of the farm of Duntulm, and at a later period of Scorrybreck in Skye. There were few gentlemen who looked better in Highland dress, and his stalwart figure seldom failed to attract attention at Highland shows. I was at the Oban bull sale in 1896, and I remember that Ensay, who was getting very stiff and heavy, was given a chair in the box beside the auctioneer. After the auctioneer had sold some of the old man's bulls, which always commanded a high price, one of his old friends came over to congratulate him on his success. Ensay was heard to remark,

" It is sad to think, Kilberry, that you and I are getting old and that we will soon have to leave the world, especially when there are so many beautiful Highland cattle in the country."

On another occasion, Ensay was in Easter Ross in connection with some sheep winterings, and remarked to a farmer that he had a good steading.

" But it will be small compared to yours, Ensay," said the man.

" Oh yes," replied the old gentleman, " the roof of my steading covers 30,000 acres "—meaning that all his stock were roaming the hills and glens of Skye and were not snugly under a roof as were the cattle of his friend in Easter Ross.

BY SEA TO OBAN.

Once when I was going with my pedigreed Highland bulls to Oban bull sale by the steamer *Claymore*, I travelled with Ensay who was on the same errand. He always travelled with his piper, who acted as valet for him, for he was now very lame and stiff with rheumatism.

Ensay's piper was descended from a race of Skye pipers almost as famous as were Rory Mhor Macleod's Macrimmons. Not only could all the male descendants of this famous family play the pipes with great skill and culture, but many of the females could also handle the *piob mhor*. It is said, indeed, that one of the elder sisters of this family used to *gleus* (tune) the pipes for her young brothers, who were unable to do it for themselves. One member of the family was piper to Queen Victoria, and when Ensay died, his piper became piper to a Highland Chieftain whom he has served faithfully for many years.

At the time of which I am speaking, it took two days to sail from Portree to Oban. Ensay's piper enlivened our voyage with his playing, and after his master had retired to his stateroom at night, a few of the younger passengers found their way to the fore part of the ship, where there were many young islanders of both sexes on their way to Glasgow.

ENTERTAINMENT ON DECK.

Our piper struck up a reel, and before long there were many willing volunteers removing hampers, lobster boxes, and other cargo until a clear space was made on deck to serve as a dance floor. The young men were soon seeking partners, but owing to the natural shyness of the Celtic temperament, they found considerable difficulty in persuading the Highland lassies, who had probably never before been so far away from their native sheilings.

Soon, however, the ice was broken, and everyone joined heartily in dancing reels, schottisches, Skye eightsomes, and the good old-fashioned polka. When the piper was in need of a rest, a call was made for a song, and a pretty young Skye lassie sang the *Skye Boat Song* in Gaelic. Then a young man sang *Clanranald's Galley*, also in Gaelic.

The next move was to get Donald, a " namely " dancer in his native glen, to dance the sword dance. The swords were provided by the cabin steward who looked out a brightly-polished set of fire-irons. Ensay's piper then struck up " Gille Challum," and Donald, clad in his homespun suit and having discarded his hobnailed boots, danced as if on air.

From the motion of the steamer it was obvious that we were approaching Ardnamurchan Point, the most westerly point of Scotland, and as some of the ladies showed signs of changing colour, the festivities were brought to a close.

ENSAY TALKS.

Next day I sat on deck with Ensay and listened with great interest while he told me of many of his varied experiences of farming and sport in the Highlands. He showed me two of the fingers of his right hand which were badly damaged, and told me that this had happened when he was a young man. He had been hunting otters with his cairn terriers and they had failed to bolt one. He removed several boulders from the cairn and succeeded in getting near the otter, but when he put his hand into the cairn, the otter immediately seized it and did not let go till he heard the bones crunching. This, Ensay said, is a characteristic of the otter—it never lets go till it hears the bones crunch.

As Ensay was a famous and skilled stocksman, I benefited greatly from my talk with him. He had a wonderful knowledge of Highland cattle, and of the management of hill farming, and he had an intense interest in Highland ponies. He bred the stallion " Skye," from whom are descended " Allan Kingsburgh " and " Rory o' the Hills " (see p. 27). The ponies of Rhum (see p. 50) are also descended from " Skye," since a brother of " Allan Kingsburgh " was used in that island by the Marquess of Salisbury.

One other characteristic of Ensay's I must mention—he spoke English with the most beautiful accent that I have ever heard, and he was also a master of pure and cultured Gaelic.

INDEX

OF PONIES, STUDS, AND PRINCIPAL BREEDERS

Names of ponies are in quotation marks.

(Part III, Reminiscences, is fully summarised on the Contents pages.)

Lightning Source UK Ltd.
Milton Keynes UK
UKOW02n0612031215

264000UK00003B/41/P